THE
FORTUNATE
YEARS

THE FORTUNATE YEARS

AN AMISH LIFE

Aaron S. Glick

Good Books

Intercourse, PA 17534

Cover illustration:
The cannery farm as painted by Aaron Glick's sister, Mary.

Design by Dawn J. Ranck

THE FORTUNATE YEARS: AN AMISH LIFE
Copyright © 1994 by Good Books
Intercourse, Pennsylvania 17534
International Standard Book Number: 1-56148-105-x
Library of Congress Catalog Card Number: 94-5073

Library of Congress Cataloging-in-Publication Data
Glick, Aaron S.
   The fortunate years : an Amish life / Aaron S. Glick.
      p. cm.
   ISBN 1-56148-105-X (pbk.) : $9.95
   1. Glick, Aaron S. 2. Amish--Pennsylvania--Lancaster
County--Social life and customs. 3. Amish--Pennsylvania--
Lancaster County--Biography. 4. Lancaster County (Pa.)--Social life and
customs. 5. Lancaster County (Pa.)--Biography. I. Title.
F457.L2G55 1994
974.8'150088287--dc20   94-5073
                                                              CIP

TABLE OF CONTENTS

Part One:
Growing Up
1903-1920

1.

Early Childhood
and
Childhood Memories

1903. Things were less complicated. The Wright Brothers were fooling around with a contraption at Kitty Hawk, but they had not yet flown. Automobiles were few and far between. Not many country people had seen one, much less had a ride in one. Telephones, radios, and televisions were somewhere off in the undreamed-of future. Scotch tape was not yet invented. There were no trucks.

Technology did not seem threatening. There was no indication that it would take control of our lives or lead to mass destruction. That's when I was born. I had little choice in the matter. But all things considered, I was fortunate in choice of parents, time, and place.

The place was Smoketown in Lancaster County, Pennsylvania. I was much too young to be aware of it, but Teddy Roosevelt, the Rough Rider Spanish American War hero, was President of the United States. His home-state politicians had maneuvered him into nomination for vice president to get him out of their way. He had made a nuisance of himself

Brothers and their dog, Tippy. Jakie, the youngest was the mechanic. Dan, the brainiest, was the natural leader. Dave, the oldest, was also the gentlest and most thoughtful. That's me on the right.

by pushing for less corruption in government, and they thought he would be out of the way as vice president. Fate decided otherwise. The assassination of President McKinley put him in the driver's seat. I suppose my parents were aware of it, but it hardly touched them. Then, as now, Amish people were non-political. Ours was an Amish family.

My deep interest in the Word of God and desire to know His will for my life I owe to a devoted Christian mother. Mother was Rebecca, daughter of David and Mary Stoltzfus

Our Smoketown birthplace.

Beiler, born in 1866. She loved the Lord. And she loved us. She had great wit and humor. I never knew her to raise her voice, even in difficult circumstances.

I was her fourth child, the third son. Mother had already learned the need for a close walk with her Lord. During all of her years, she spent much of her thought life in quiet meditation, especially during her working hours. She had almost no leisure since most of her time was needed for homemaking and the care of her children.

My father, Isaac Neuhauser Glick, was a cripple. A stiff, weak leg made it impossible for him to do ordinary farm work so he had to find other ways to earn a living. After a few years of trying to farm, he developed a plant and seed business. Here his physical handicap created fewer problems.

Mother cared for the garden, growing vegetables for the family table. She made clothing for the entire family, using a treadle sewing machine. She had one modern appliance—a washing machine operated by a belt-driven line shaft and powered by a gasoline engine. (Dad also used the gasoline engine to run the pump for watering the greenhouse plants.) She ironed with flat irons heated on the kitchen range for which we children would carry the wood or coal.

Mother had the help of my sisters, Malinda and Mary. Malinda's mother died at childbirth so my mother became mother to her when she became my father's second wife. Mother usually had a hired man to feed in addition to the family. Customers who came to buy plants or seeds at mealtime also were invited to eat with us. I never knew Mother to complain about the unexpected guests. In fact, I don't remember that she ever complained at all.

She baked the best bread and churned butter from the cream of several cows. I was often "permitted" to do the churning. I recall the delicious buttermilk, a real reward for my job. Mother also helped to prepare garden produce for the street market stand that Dad and my older brothers ran in Lancaster, as well as for a stand in the Northern Market at the corner of Queen Street and Walnut Street.

With all that Mother had to do, she still found time for her most important task. Mother first taught us the ABC's in German, and then taught us to read the Gospels verse by verse. We little fellows would often sit on the lower stairstep as Mother prepared a meal or sewed busily. She was able to supervise our Bible reading without looking at the book or interrupting her work. When we stumbled on a word, she corrected us so we could read on. She taught us reverence for the Word of God.

My Mother's Family

Mother was the ninth child in a family of twelve children. Her father, the second David Beiler, was a minister, and her grandfather, the first David Beiler (1786-1866), was an Amish bishop, an influential church leader, and a man whose counsel was valued by the ministry of distant Amish congregations. He wrote several books. One, *Das Wahre Christenthum*, was reprinted in the 1980s. David Beiler's writings indicate a concern for the church and the coming generations. His accounts exhibit conservative thought

7

and record some of the astonishing changes in lifestyle which he observed.

To him, many of the changes seemed evidence of a growing pride. The coming of the Industrial Revolution was making life easier for many people. David Beiler wrote that Amish people of his youth wore clothes made of homespun linen even "for Sunday," and that it had not been a practice to wear bright-colored shirts of "finer" material. Great-grandfather Beiler also wrote that folks walked miles to worship services, barefooted. Shoes were only for winter.

He explained that mothers and their daughters spent their winter evenings spinning flax and wool to make the yarn which they then wove into cloth to clothe the family. Writing as a mature old man, he remembered the hum of the spinning wheels as music. The flax was grown on the farm, harvested, retted, broken, cleaned, and hackled in preparation for spinning. For thousands of years spinning was a near-religious task for the womenfolk. That came to an end with the coming of factory-made cotton cloth.

If he was conscious of the political world around him, Great-grandfather Beiler didn't write about it. It seems a pity. It would be nice to know how he and his family felt about the struggling early days of the thirteen United States. Born in 1786 before George Washington was elected president, he was 26 years old at the start of the War of 1812. He would have been old enough to vote when John Adams was elected President. But politics probably seemed an evil preoccupation to him. His citizenship was firmly in the Heavenly Kingdom, not in the secular world around him. His wife, my great-grandmother, Elizabeth Fisher, and his father, Christian Beiler, were first-generation Americans. David Beiler was approaching middle age before there were railroads or reapers or threshing machines or covered bridges in Pennsylvania.

The Amish society of his generation was a tiny fragment of the refugees from Switzerland who came by way of Germany and the Alsace of France. Their first community on the

My maternal grandmother, Mary Stoltzfus Beiler, owned this **Taufschein** (Baptismal Certificate).

Northkill Creek in Berks County, Pennsylvania, was uprooted by Indian massacres during the French and Indian War. By the time Great-grandfather was growing up after the Revolutionary War, the group had dispersed in several directions with a growing settlement in Lancaster County.

✦ ✦ ✦

My maternal grandmother, Mary Stoltzfus Beiler (David Beiler, Sr.'s daughter-in-law), was one of the fourteen children of "Tennessee" John and Catherine Hooley Stoltzfus. She cooked over an open fire in the fireplace when she and Grandfather were first married. Of course she got an iron kitchen range in due time. But not every household had a cookstove in the early 1800s.

Grandmother Beiler, as I remember her, was a small aged lady sitting on her rocking chair with her knitting. I don't remember that she was talkative, but I was only a youngster when she passed away at 95 in 1916.

Her parents and most of the family moved to Concord, Tennessee, in 1871. By then, she had married David Beiler Jr., a minister in the Old Order Amish Church, so she stayed in Pennsylvania.

The children of Catherine Hooley were sometimes described by their grandchildren as very determined people. Others have referred to the "Hooley streak of stubborness," perhaps unjustly. My grandmother was evidently a strict disciplinarian with her own family, but as a teenager, we think she was vivacious and less committed to church rules.

I have Grandmother's *Taufschein* (Baptismal Certificate) which states, "*Gebaren den 20 tag June 1827, und getauft den 17ten September 1843*" (Born June 20, 1827, and baptized September 17, 1843). The certificate includes a poem expressing the joy of the experience. It is a certificate of the kind that were printed in Reading and Harrisburg by the hundreds if not thousands, mainly for the "Church" people, that is, the Lutheran and Reformed Germans who previously had used hand-painted fraktur certificates. The printed certificates had a pair of angels and blank lines where ministers entered the correct names and dates. They would normally have been given to parents when children were baptized as infants.

I have one particularly vivid memory of Grandmother Beiler. Mother sent me to her house for healing because I had a sty in one eye. She took a shovel of live coals from the fire in the

The log house of "Indian" John Glick.

stove. She passed the shovel from the center of the front of my head to the center of the back of my head, repeating it several times and saying a prayer-charm. I stayed at her house several days so she did the treatment each day.

Today people aren't comfortable talking about this part of our Amish past. But the *Braucheri* healing was also part of our heritage. The name or term may derive from the Hebrew or Yiddish *Baruch*, meaning "to bless." It was not a black art or witchcraft. The charms are very old and probably predate the Reformation.

Grandmother Beiler's family was renowned for longevity. When her youngest brother died in 1949, he was buried at the Millwood Cemetery near Gap, Pennsylvania. The first person buried at Millwood had been his infant sister who had passed away 103 years earlier. He was in his 96th year. He had daughters and nieces who outlived him. One of his daughters passed away at 103.

Time Out for the Indians

The Mifflin County, Belleville community is thought of as the ancestral home of the Glicks. There is little detailed information on the first generation and almost none of their origin in Europe. It appears that a family headed by a Peter Glick arrived in what is now Berks County north of Reading near the Blue Mountain about 1747.

Peter Glick may have been a weaver by trade. It isn't clear if he was Amish or Lutheran. He took out a warrant for land on what was then known as "Greenbrier Creek along the road that leads to Shamokin," but didn't settle there. The Indians made the move unnecessary.

It was during the French and Indian War in 1756, and the natives were making raids across Blue Mountain. They struck the Glick cabin and burned it in the night, killing the people as they ran out to escape the flames. Cabins were burning all along the frontier.

The famed Hostetler massacre also took place around this time. People were fleeing to the safer settlements behind the frontier. According to one tradition, the Peter Glick family was packed and ready to leave. A small child, little Johnnie, was sent with the neighbors, who left a day earlier, because the Glick family was large and their wagon would be full. The Glicks stayed one more night; the night they were struck.

There may have been other survivors, but if so they apparently never made contact with their little brother. In Conrad Weiser's report to Goverener Denny, he lists one massacre that seems to fit the circumstances of the Glick family. That report lists both killed and wounded. A hundred years later the Reading Eagle almanac reported on the Glick massacre, but does not really add to our information. Young Johnny Glick was apparently raised by foster parents. We do not have information on their identity. They may have been Amish.

An account of the settlement of Peter Glick's estate is found on page 100 of the first volume of estate settlements in the courthouse in Reading. The executor was a man named Rotharmel, meaning "redsleeves" in German, which is not an Amish or Mennonite name. If Peter Glick was Amish, his executor was not.

In any case, Indian John Glick (as he came to be called)

was an Amishman living in Mifflin County not far from Belleville by the time we find him as an adult. One of his younger sons, David, became my great-grandfather. David's wife was a girl named Magdalena Lantz. We aren't sure of the identity of Indian John's wife.

A number of John Glick's children are buried in the Amish cemetery near Allensville. There is an old stone nearby with the initials, J.G. We don't know if this is John Glick's resting place or that of his son John, Jr. There is another cemetery on the hill in a field owned by the Glicks that is thought to be the resting place of John and his wife. But it is hardly certain. The date given for the death of Mrs. John Glick is several years prior to the birth of her youngest children. Something may have been overlooked.

David, my great-grandfather, and his brother Sam married two of the three Lantz sisters. David and Sam Glick lived in the Buffalo Valley west of Lewisburg. When the Amish church there disintegrated, David and his wife, Magdalena, moved to Lancaster County. They are buried in the Myers Cemetery near the New Holland Pike.

One of Indian John Glick's sons went west to Indiana. His son trekked on west to Iowa where he became the father of Anna Glick, the woman who would become my wife.

✦ ✦ ✦

My paternal grandfather, Christian F., son of David and Magdalena Lantz Glick, was born April 22, 1846. He married Barbara Neuhauser on February 1, 1870. Barbara died January 16, 1873, several weeks after my father, Isaac, was born. Christian Glick later married Lydia Hertzler. Meanwhile, he had handed his small son, Isaac, over to his sister and her husband, Michael Beiler, who adopted and raised Isaac as their own son.

Grandfather Glick and his second family lived at Academia, Juniata County, Pennsylvania. Later they lived in Buffalo Valley in Union County. When that group disbanded, they moved to Bealton, Virginia, on New Year's Day, 1900. They were one of the first Amish families to locate in the Norfolk,

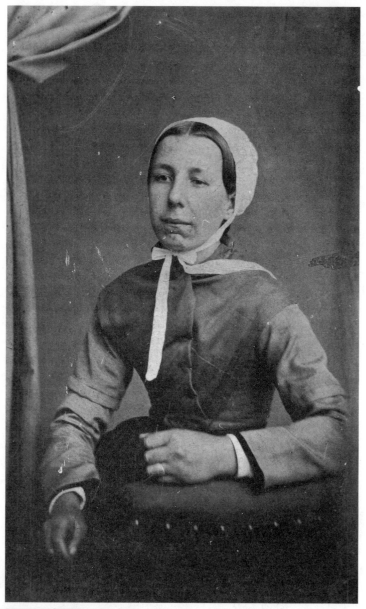

My grandmother, Barbara Neuhauser Glick. She died soon after my father, Isaac, was born.

My grandfather Christian Glick. After asking his sister to take care of his infant son, Isaac, Grandfather Glick remarried and raised another family. He seldom visited us.

Virginia, area. Later Grandfather Glick joined the Amish Mennonite group at Fentress, Virginia. Several of his children eventually moved to eastern Montana and homesteaded north of Glendive.

Grandfather Glick rarely visited us. The last time was early in March, 1913. I was so taken up by our forthcoming school program that I insisted he stay for this. But he said no and left for Virginia. He took sick with pneumonia and died before our school program. He was buried at Fentress, Virginia.

Growing Up in an Amish Family

As was the custom, our Amish church district gathered for a worship service every other Sunday. On the off Sunday, we spent time together as a family reading the Bible in German. It was like a little Sunday school. I remember one time when I was thought to be too young to understand. I was playing with blocks and Dad was explaining Nicodemus's visit to Jesus by night in John 3 to my older brothers, Dan and David. How well I still remember that time. My hands were playing with blocks but my ears weren't.

On the Sunday mornings when we had church, we all had to get up early to do our barn chores and have breakfast in time to get washed and dressed. We were usually instructed to wash our necks and ears in spite of the fact that we had had a tub bath the evening before. This was the only time in the week that we wore white shirts. David, Dan, and Malinda usually went in the open buggy, but Mary, Jacob, and I went in the carriage (the *Dachwegli*) with our parents.

I don't remember that sister Annie, next youngest, ever went along to worship, but of course she did. She died on May 14, 1910, when she was five years old. She had been a frail child. I think she had pneumonia when quite young and was weakened from that. I remember when she was sick in bed in her little crib. Our parents had gone to Lancaster to do some shopping. They bought a pair of little rubber overshoes for Annie. They tied a twine across the top of the crib and hung the two rubbers from it. Annie was so happy to have those rubbers. She never wore them. When summer came, her spirit had fled. While I remember the funeral at home, I don't recall going along to the cemetery.

Our family home life would have been considered fairly normal. Each growing child had some work to do. Quite young, I was given the responsibility of caring for some livestock. Every year we raised several pigs to be butchered after New Year's Day. This provided meat for the coming year. One of my unsupervised tasks was to feed the pigs until they became hogs. I recall one year at butchering time we had three hogs to dress. One pen had one hog and the other pen had two hogs. Dad said that by the looks of the hogs, each pen must have been given the same amount of feed. I had indeed prepared and fed one bucket of slop to each pen. The next year my sister Malinda fed the pigs.

We also had several registered Guernsey cows and heifers. It was my job to feed and care for these animals, also to pasture them. One of my sisters usually did the milking and cared for the cream separator. The cream was either churned or sold as cream to an ice cream maker in Lancaster.

For a refrigerator we had a dumbwaiter. It was something like a refrigerator with shelves that were balanced with a weight on the end of a rope. It could be lowered down into a dry well just beneath the kitchen for cooling.

✦ ✦ ✦

There was no shortage of fine baked things before the invention of the kitchen range. The dome-shaped brick bake oven baked the bread and pies before the coming of the iron stove. Sometimes these ovens were separate free-standing structures or were built into the kettle house or summer kitchen. Ours was built into one end of the basement. To use it, we first built a fire right in the oven to heat the bricks to baking temperature. When the oven was hot, the ashes of the fire were raked out. Baking came next. The retained heat in the bricks baked the bread and pies and cooked the roasts and other food. In the fall, the oven was filled with ears of corn when the baking was finished. The leftover heat dried and roasted the corn which was then shelled and taken to the mill to be ground into cornmeal, an important item in our winter diet.

The oven was too hot for bread when the fire was first raked out. If cookies were to be baked, they went in first because they could be baked at higher temperatures. My wife, Anna, used to judge the baking heat by thrusting her arm into the oven and counting to 39. If the oven was so hot that she couldn't stand the heat, it was too hot for the bread. That was before the day of oven thermometers. A long-handled flat iron shovel was used to place the baking pans into the oven. Pies and cakes went into the oven after the bread was baked. The oven retained the heat a long while.

✦ ✦ ✦

As a very small child, I would tell my mother my childish longings. One day I told her I would like to have a sea, meaning, of course, a pond. She asked where I would like to have my sea? "Oh," I said, "just here back of the house."

We had a number of cats in the stable and we children usually had a name for each one. Mother never paid too much attention to our cat names. But one cat given a female name grew fairly large and one day Mother suggested, "Better call the cat Jack." So we renamed the cat. Later Mother was amused when one of us children rushed in to tell her that Jack had a kitten. So Mother suggested we rename the cat again.

Mary, Jacob, and I would play in the apple orchard, just north of the house where we also pastured some heifers. How we played. We each had a play farm. We laid the boundaries for our farms with sticks and the remains of the rockets, Roman candles, and other tubes that we collected from our neighbors after they had their fireworks on July 4th. The Fourth of July celebrations were not exactly safe and sane. Folks would sometimes lose fingers if these rockets exploded in their hands. We never invested in the fireworks.

I remember once in our play farm experience that sister Mary had running water on her farm furnished by her pet Guernsey calf, who just stepped into her farm. The heifer's name was Martha.

My brother Dan and I were responsible to keep the horse stable swept daily. For this we received ten cents a week. It happened that on my week I once forgot to do it, so the next day I swept the stable twice to make up for the day I missed. As a lad I remember leading a horse to the stable when I was barefoot. The horse tramped on my foot. I cried, perhaps too loudly, so Dad called out from the house that if I didn't stop it, he would come out and give me something to cry about. I got the message.

✦ ✦ ✦

Even though Dad was a cripple, he had a keen mind. Amish homes in general had no indoor plumbing, but Dad was years ahead of many others. He had a water tank put into the room above the kitchen. He had the rain water from the roof of the main house spouted into it. I still remember the sound of the water flowing into the tank during an all-night rain. How very soothing! The weekly bath was usually taken behind the kitchen stove in a large size washtub.

For the most part, any hot water needed in the household was heated on the kitchen range. Water for washing dishes, scrubbing floors, and Saturday night baths was brought into the kitchen in a bucket from the cistern, the tank (rain water), or from the pump at the well. For doing laundry, water was often heated in a large walled-in iron kettle in the kettle house adjacent to the kitchen.

The woodshed was next to the kettle house. Firewood, cut to the right length and split, was stored there for the kitchen range. The woodshed was where Dad would find a stick if he needed to correct any of us. The privy was built in at the end of the woodshed. Flush-type indoor toilets were not known in the countryside.

Ordinarily, the kitchen was the only heated room in the house during the winter. The room directly above the kitchen was partly warmed by the kitchen stovepipe that passed through it to the chimney in the attic. That room was the *ruhr stub* or the stovepipe room. There was a heating stove in the living room that was usually fired up for weekends. It, too, provided some heat for the bedroom above. On the coldest mid-winter nights one would sometimes heat a brick on the kitchen range. This was wrapped in newspapers and taken along to bed as a foot warmer. With a double blanket and a thick "comfort" it was possible to sleep warm and cozy. Sometimes a small bag of shelled corn was warmed to use instead of a brick. Either worked real well.

We slept on rope beds. Instead of springs, beds were supported by a long rope that was laced end-to-end and crosswise to support the mattress—a large "chaff bag" filled with straw cut to about four-inch lengths. The straw was replaced annually with straw cut by a manually operated straw cutter. Sometimes corn husks substituted for straw to fill the chaff bags. For this, husks were gathered after corn husking. The butt ends of the husks were cut off on a block with a sharp hatchet before the husks were chopped. It was a lot of work for the housewives but was part of the fall housecleaning routine. The chaff bags were shook up each morning when beds were made so the bed would be nice and level for the next night.

✦ ✦ ✦

Mother never turned away any road walker who came asking for food. We called them tramps. They would usually sleep in the stable feedway where it was warm. They were asked to leave their matches in the house. Mother gave them food. Sometimes she would ask them to split some wood for the meal.

One, a fellow named Tom Clark, carried a satchel of small items such as shoe strings, safety pins, and the like which he sold. We called him the safety pin man. He would always say to us little boys, "God bless you my boy." I was a bit awed as a child. I remember that one evening as he was bedded down for the night in the feedway, we heard him humming to himself. I insisted he was praying. My older brothers laughed at my idea.

I also remember a man named John Booth. My brother Jakie was very friendly with him. He helped him make his bed in the barn haymow. I insisted that Jake stop being so friendly because John Booth came too often.

Amish Meeting

It was always a special experience to go to Sunday morning worship. Meetings were always held in a member's home. Most of the furniture was removed before meeting day. Backless benches were placed in rows in all the downstairs rooms. When we were on the way to the farm where services were to be conducted, there were usually several carriages going the same way; it was sort of an unwritten law that one never passed the others. Upon arriving, the womenfolk got off at the yard gate in front of the house. Then we would proceed to the back of the barn, unhitch the horse, and find room to tie him beside the other horses, usually in the barn floor adjoining the haymow. Sometimes the barn was so filled with horses that it was almost necessary to crawl out over the backs of the other horses tied there. Then, too, there was some danger of being kicked by the spirited horses.

It would be unfair not to mention the lunch that was provided after worship services—the snitz pie and apple pie (in apple season). I never had much appreciation for the apple pie. Since we had to eat it with our hands, it could be rather messy. Sometimes we had homemade buns and cheese with this, and of course coffee, pickles, red beets, honey, and jelly. No plates were used. Only a knife, a spoon, a glass for water, and a coffee cup were provided for each person.

I remember one occasion, after worship services, some of us 12-14-year-old boys were to eat first because a neighbor's small child had died and we were to *hostler* (take care of the horses in the afternoon at the funeral). When we sat down to eat, and after saying grace as was the custom, the younger teenage girls waited on the table. As I held out my cup for some coffee, the girl serving me missed her aim for the cup and poured the hot coffee on my wrist. Needless to say, I pulled my arm back rather suddenly, and she found herself pouring coffee on the bench. I was probably impolite because the coffee was very hot.

2.

The Accident
and
Dad's Businesses

Our father, Isaac Neuhauser Glick, was crippled. One of his knees had been injured in an accident during his first year in school. Some of the bigger boys were running around the schoolhouse in a game of "gunner." Not seeing the little Amish boy around the corner, one ran over him. His knee-cap was knocked out of place. The local doctor felt that Dad's knee would get better in a short time. It never did. Because of the sore leg someone got him a brace for his knee. This relieved some of the strain. But he had pain in his crippled leg most of the time. It was not until his leg was amputated that they discovered his knee socket had been cracked and never healed. This had left his left leg deformed and weak.

In the fall of 1909 as the fodder shredder was pulling into our driveway to set up on the barn hill, Father hurried out and slipped on the cement walk. He put the left leg forward to keep from falling, and this broke the bone about three inches above the knee.

Dr. Atlee discovered the leg was too weak and the bone

23

too brittle to set the break. He tried to set Dad's break three times but couldn't do a satisfactory job, so he decided to amputate the leg. This was done at our home on the dining room table. I remember seeing them carry my father's leg out. We children were in the next room. I was six years old.

✦ ✦ ✦

The matter of earning a living in spite of his handicap was something Father had to learn, unexpectedly, at an early age. Since his mother died soon after his birth, he was given a home with a childless, elderly aunt and uncle. The uncle, Michael Beiler, was a farmer, carpenter, and Amish undertaker. He made coffins and used his spring wagon as the hearse.

Uncle Mike, who had given Dad a home from birth, had specified in his will that Dad was to have a life-right on the 19-acre Smoketown farm, but he was also to provide for Aunt Catherine—Uncle Mike's widow—from the farm's produce. Uncle Mike's will detailed things he was to provide that took most, if not all, of the farm's income and made it difficult for Dad to meet any other obligations since he did not have the off-farm income of his cabinetmaker uncle. For Uncle Mike the farm was little more than a sideline.

It was difficult for Dad to do the farming with a weak knee. His only harrow was a spike harrow. Spring tooth harrows and disk harrows were as yet unknown. Few implements had seats. One walked behind the horses. Farming was hard work for the strong and too much for the handicapped.

Dad's first wife, Malinda, died following the birth of Malinda, their first child. When Dad was a widower with his little baby Malinda to care for, his cousins, the Jacob R. Glicks, came and lived with Dad and cared for him and his baby daughter until he married Mother. About this time Jake's first wife died, too. These events brought both men very close together. Their first wives had been sisters. While Dad and Jake were cousins, they functioned as brothers. We considered cousin Jacob an uncle, always calling him Uncle Jake.

GROWING UP—1903-1920

✦ ✦ ✦

During my father's early farming years, it was customary to buy feed at the mill and food at the grocery store with settlement to be made on April 1st for the preceding year. The farmer would take his wheat to the feed mill; his butter and eggs to the grocery store. Every rural home had a few chickens. Groceries at the store, as well as feed needs at the mill, were about balanced at the end of the year. Grocery needs were few around 1900.

Because Dad was having difficulty paying his balance, the local feed miller decided to cut off his credit, so he told his helper, Jacob Fisher, "When that lame Amishman comes again for feed, don't give him anything unless he has the cash to pay." When the helper saw Dad coming, he hid to avoid the embarrassment of refusing to serve Father. The owner waited on Dad, gave him feed, and put it on the charge account. Years later Jacob Fisher told Dad the dilemma.

Dad sometimes found himself unable to meet his April 1st payments. In the meantime, we children were born, and something had to be done. So Dad conceived the idea of having a farm auction each spring. He had a few vegetable plants transplanted for this sale as he had a small green-house. He also had some new garden tools, as well as some farm and garden seeds and three or four cows that would freshen by sale day. Dad would also buy some horses, and with the help of Ike Kennel, his cousin who worked for him, have them broken to be sold at the sale. I remember they used to plait the manes and tails several days before sale, opening the plait the morning of the sale. I think sometimes they also tied small blue ribbons in the horses' manes.

Dad found he could buy at regular farm auctions with ten months or a year to pay. So he bought his livestock this way and was able to have his own sale for cash and have the use of the money for the balance of the year. At one time, about 1909, he and Uncle Jacob R. Glick bought a carload of horses in Holmes County, Ohio, brought them to the farm, and had a horse sale.

25

✦ ✦ ✦

Also around 1909 Dad's vegetable plant business on the Smoketown farm developed. He needed a building. The one he designed was energy-efficient and economical. Partly earth-sheltered, its south face was glassed to serve as a greenhouse. It was used for many years by what became Glick's Plant Farm. The north part of the building was enclosed and used for storage, an office, and a salesroom for farm field seeds. This part of the business grew so rapidly that by 1910 another building was built nearer to the road. Later used as a dwelling, this building was also used for the Post Office and for what became the P.L. Rohrer Seed business.

The greenhouse work included growing acres of vegetable plants, mostly cabbage. These plants were shipped by express in crates constructed out of light bass wood. Large orders like 100,000 cabbage plants went to New York State. I remember orders from the Skaneateles Kraut Co. Dad had one order for one million plants. These had to be dug with wheel hoe diggers and counted in bunches. This gave a lot of employment to local folks. Many Amish as well as others benefitted from this employment. The winter seedling transplanting in the greenhouse also required hiring local workers until the shipped, southern plants came on the market. Dad experimented with having plants grown earlier, outdoors, by an Amishman in Dover, Delaware, and by another grower in Virginia.

Day-Old Chick Business

Dad was also a pioneer in the baby chick hatching business. At this time people usually had chickens—any color, black and white and speckled and brown, but always mixed, just a barnyard flock. I don't recall ever seeing any green chickens, to be sure, but I believe I saw every other color. It occurred to Dad that it would be a good idea to hatch and sell day-old chicks, since they could be sold before they had a chance to get sick. Chicks didn't need any feed for the first 24-36 hours, a good time to move them. He had twelve

A modern incubator.

400-egg incubators heated with kerosene lamps. The eggs were on trays; two wire trays to a machine. I think he had two rows of six machines in the basement of the brooder house and a 3000-egg unit in the basement of the building he built for all-purpose work. The egg trays needed to be removed from the incubators daily. Each egg had to be turned in the morning just as a setting hen turned her eggs by walking around on them as she moved on and off her nest. This was a job for the boys.

Sometimes an egg was cracked during handling the first day, and it was then laid out on the incubator. Many times when eggs were cracked, we took them to the house to eat. But you guessed it, once in a while an egg with a chick inside got mixed with the good eggs. Imagine the surprise on breaking an egg open on your plate for breakfast and finding a chicken eye looking at you.

Hired man Pete Kennel assisted Dad in many ways, and

one of his contributions included seeing to it that we boys helped with the work of the hatchery. These were the days before New Castle and kindred poultry diseases. Dad shipped the day-old chicks to buyers by express, mostly east of the Mississippi, though he once made a shipment as far away as Texas.

Dad used to have farmers grow flocks of purebred chickens so he would have a good supply of eggs. We raised many pullets, or so I thought. Once, at mealtime, we saw that one of the colony houses, used to grow chickens on range, had caught fire. The kerosene lamp that was used for heating the colony house must have started it. Pete Kennel grabbed a large cooling can of fresh milk and dashed it on the fire. I was impressed. When the chick business became large enough to be a separate business, it was sold to Elwood Hershey. Hershey let the business decline in the years shortly before and during World War I, when it was possible to earn higher wages in defense work.

The Field Seed Business

Dad's field seed business was eventually taken over by Pete Rohrer. Today it is still called the P.L. Rohrer & Brother Seed Company. As I remember it, Dad had a garden catalog printed and distributed about 1905. It had pretty pictures, as garden catalogs have. This was his first attempt. The second attempt, the next year, consisted of only a few pages. He was learning the hard way, but it was real learning.

The catalog listed articles other than seeds such as bone cutters used to make bone meal for poultry, small incubators, and the prominent seed cleaner made by Jonas B. Reist and Son of Harrisburg, Pennsylvania. Dad sold quite a few of these seed cleaners to farmers, especially when he demonstrated the machine. At that time much small grain was grown, and the farmer planted his own seed, which needed cleaning.

The catalog also included moth traps that cost a dollar. The trap was a large shallow pan, in which a kerosene lamp was placed at night. As the moths were attracted to the light, they would fall into the liquid placed around the lamp. It was thought that the traps would destroy the moths that damaged tobacco. But the tobacco worm moths ignored the traps. Buyers called them dollar catchers because they didn't catch the tobacco worm moths as effectively as other moths. The entire reason for purchase was to control the tobacco moths. The buyers weren't interested in other moths. That effort was short-lived.

Dad's interest turned more and more to the area of vegetable plants. He began to ship plants by parcel post and developed a large mail order business. This naturally included hauling the plants to the Bird-in-Hand Post Office, which required valuable time. For this, a horse was pressed into service. Dad believed the situation would be improved by obtaining a post office for Smoketown. How this came about must include the introduction of another Smoketown personality.

The Doctor's Help

A young doctor, Donald McCaskey, lived at the west end of Smoketown where the East Lampeter School is located now. As young doctors go, he also had a lot of what was known as "head knowledge." He had many good ideas, but as a city boy some were not considered too practical by his country neighbors. Among other things, he owned a Buick— one of those new fangled things in which the driver sat way up there. It had no windshield; goggles served for that. No windshield wipers were needed either because goggles can be wiped by your forearm.

Donald McCaskey also had a dog and when he came down the road, he would put his dog on the back end of the car (not yet developed into a trunk). One day the dog fell off, so he stopped promptly and helped the dog back on with the rebuke, "You must learn to hold on!"

Dr. McCaskey saved John Denlinger's life when his arm was badly shot up by his own shotgun while he was crossing a fence. The doctor rushed him to the hospital in his Buick, probably at the top speed of 25 miles per hour.

An unusual Smoketown personality, Dr. Donald McCaskey, and his "baby" Buick.

An unfortunate episode practically ruined the doctor's practice. It happened that a mother who brought him her child with a cold was advised to bathe its feet in hot water. He emphasized that the water be hot, and the poor woman scalded the child's feet. Of course, the mother should have used common sense and not have scalded the child's feet.

The doctor had a new furnace, but could not heat his house. He called Dad in to see what was wrong. Dad noticed he had the damper in the stovepipe open. So he asked Dr. McCaskey whether he wanted to heat the township or his home. The doctor took the hint and closed the damper and easily heated his home thereafter.

Being a "community man" the doctor decided to try out the response time of the local Witmer Fire Company when they obtained their new engine. So he made a huge pile of locust fenceposts directly behind his barn and set them on fire to see if they could come quickly. But when the firemen came down the Witmer road and saw the fire was behind the barn instead of in it, they pulled under the neighbor's barn forebay and let the doctor's locust posts burn up. He was disappointed.

The doctor also saw the need for better roads. The Old Philadelphia Pike, now Route 340, was a one-way track consisting of ruts that the heavy iron-tired wagons followed to haul produce to Lancaster. No blacktop was known in that day. So the doctor advocated the use of the King drag. This was a special horse-drawn drag used to grade dirt roads. He did much to make our mud roads better. He had himself elected Road Supervisor. Then, as always, some folks rejected new ways because of the expense involved, and the doctor made enemies through his good-roads effort. For obvious reasons, he was also never very successful as a country doctor.

However, Dr. McCaskey did Dad a lot of good. He helped Dad learn to write business letters correctly and taught him other things about business. It was Dr. McCaskey who suggested to Dad, "Why not get a post office for Smoketown?" So with the doctor's help and coaching, Dad went to work

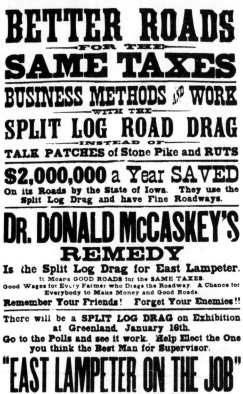

(top) A badly rutted road in Lancaster County at the turn of the century.

(left) An advertisement for Dr. Donald McCaskey's split log road drag. Dr. McCaskey worked diligently to improve road conditions in the early 1900s.

on the idea. Early one morning he set out and called on all the folks in Smoketown to have them sign a petition for a post office. Before anyone had time to think much about it, Dad had all the signatures.

Some people expressed objections to the idea later, but their names were on the list. Things moved rather slowly, so one day the doctor called the assistant postmaster general in Washington, DC and let him know that this thing was urgent. A long distance call to Washington, DC was almost unheard of then.

W.W. Griest was our local congressman at the time. He also helped get the post office. It put Smoketown on the map. It was 1912 and Dad served as postmaster until World War I. When Dad resigned, the Rohrers had it for many years.

◆ ◆ ◆

The post office was a more important event for us youngsters than the turmoil of the world beyond Smoketown. Democrat Woodrow Wilson was elected president in 1912 because the Republicans goofed. William Howard Taft had replaced Teddy Roosevelt in 1908 as Roosevelt's hand-picked successor. But Taft made the mistake of thinking for himself after the election. Roosevelt seems to have expected to call the shots. When that didn't happen, he threw his hat in the ring in 1912, running against both Taft and Wilson. He called his splinter group the Bull Moose Republicans. By splitting the Republican vote, Roosevelt gave the election to Wilson who would have lost if the Republicans had been united on a single candidate.

During a Lancaster whistle-stop, Teddy Roosevelt gave a campaign address from the Hotel Brunswick balcony across from the old Pennsylvania Railroad Station. There he was introduced to my mother's cousin, Ezra Stoltzfus, from the Gap. Ezra was an Amishman with a beard, running for state legislature on Roosevelt's Bull Moose ticket.

"Hooray," Teddy supposedly said, "we will have 'Old Dutch Cleanser' in this campaign." The trademark on Old Dutch

Cleanser packages in those days was a picture of a Dutch woman chasing dirt. All for naught. Woodrow Wilson was elected president. And Ezra, the would-be politician, was estranged from the Amish church because of his runaway political ambition. Then, as now, Amish society considered politics inappropriate for Christians. Roosevelt may or may not have been right about Taft. President Taft left little mark on American society and is remembered mostly for the jokes people made about him. One that made the rounds was based on his love for good food and his resulting weight problem. The story went that, in spite of being overweight, President Taft was nevertheless courteous and polite. In fact, on a streetcar one day, he stood up and gave his seat to a small group of ladies.

✦ ✦ ✦

There was an event in 1912 that did get wide attention, even in Smoketown. The new, unsinkable steamship *Titanic* hit an iceberg and sank on her maiden voyage across the Atlantic. More than 1000 people drowned. In the far-off Balkans they were shooting at each other in what would become a world war, but we weren't much aware of it.

The Constable's Visit

One day while Dad was postmaster, a business man came into his office. He didn't say what his errand was, and his manner was close to arrogance. Dad was a bit impatient by the man's intrusive manner and asked, "Well, do you have a search warrant for me?"

"No," the man said quickly, "but I have another warrant." Here was the Constable Steigerwalt with a warrant for an unnamed lame Amishman. The constable soon realized that Dad wasn't the man he was looking for. It seems that someone's horse-drawn wagon had scraped a car, and the owner was upset. I don't know how it turned out, but my father's wagon had not been involved.

3.

Transportation in the Early 1900s

The Fire Company

While firefighting equipment was virtually nonexistent outside the cities before World War I, our nearby small village of Witmer formed a volunteer fire company in 1910. We had a chemical fire extinguisher tank and a horse-drawn fire engine. When a fire was discovered, Fire Chief J.Z. Beiler would hitch his horses to the engine and drive like "Jehu" to get to the fire. One time one of his horses was overheated and, due to lack of proper care while Beiler was fighting the fire, contracted pneumonia and died.

The first trustees of this volunteer fire company were J.Z. Beiler, Adam Miller Witmer, and my father, I.N. Glick, of Smoketown. The original charter hangs in the present-day Witmer Fire Hall.

The first Witmer Fire Hall was built near the train station. The cost of the building and additional equipment was partly met by donations from Lancaster businessmen, who largely

The old Witmer firehouse by the railroad bridge.

depended on the rural folks for their business. Dad contacted these men by letter. The response was satisfactory.

At one of the quarterly meetings, my father suggested that a better or faster way was needed to get to fires: a motor vehicle. A motion was made and seconded to look into this, and a Model T Ford touring car was purchased from neighbor Jake Fisher. This was stripped and the fire engine was mounted on it. It consisted of two chemical tanks that got their pressure through a mixture of soda and acid. Now we were really equipped to fight fires! We even went so far as the village of Intercourse when George Beiler's barn burned down at threshing time in 1919.

Today this engine might be an amusing antique, but in its day it filled a need. It was my brother David's responsibility to drive the Model T Ford fire engine occasionally to see that it was in good working order and ready to go. How he enjoyed that!

Early Autos

In my early years, the automobile was a rarity. Many different descriptions existed. I remember something that looked like a buggy with high wheels and had solid rubber tires. Its engine was under the seat. Tires were a problem, complicated by bad roads. There were many flats.

Most people thought cars would never become a common thing. In winter the car was usually put on blocks to hibernate. Because of bad road conditions in the spring, some people waited and got only a half-year license for their car. The sight of a car going down the road was a novelty. We children often screamed "auto-know-better," telling the others a car was going by.

The first auto ride that I can recall was provided by William Cosner in 1915 in a Dodge touring car with several of my brothers. We traveled from Kreider's Store at Witmer via the Horseshoe Road, to his house at Witmer Heights, across from what is now the First Deaf Mennonite Church. We gave him twenty-five cents for the ride. It was about three miles.

These gas buggies frightened horses. Folks were afraid the horse would bolt and run away when they met a car. At farm sales a driving horse was often advertised as "not afraid of automobiles," and such a horse brought real money. But as time went on, cars became more and more plentiful, and the horses learned to ignore them.

It was the Model T Ford that made transportation by car available for the average person. While folks laughed at the "Tin Lizzie," it was popular and was built from 1908 to 1927 with only minor changes in body style and in such luxuries as a self-starter to replace the crank. It was common for the motor to kick when cranked, and sometimes an arm would be broken when this happened. After Ford introduced assembly-line manufacturing around 1912, cars became

Our son Ivan and his 1921 Model T touring car in 1947.

rather plentiful. While cars were no longer a novelty, it was not until about 1918-19 that the Mellinger Church Mennonites "put away" their horses and started using cars.

The Model T Ford touring car did not have a trunk so the running board was used to haul things. One day my wife's uncle, Milton Brenneman, was taking a coop of half-grown leghorn roosters from Kalona to the Iowa City market. The coop was tied to the left running board. At a bend in the road another motorist passed him too closely and ripped open the coop and the roosters flew in every direction. Uncle Milton "allowed" the motorist to help catch all the roosters, so this was not a hit-and-run accident after all.

My brother, Jake, and the Model T Ford both saw the light of day at around the same time. And for Jake, a natural-born mechanic, it was close to a love affair throughout his growing-up years. He took to Fords. And years after the Model T gave way to the Model A and V-8's, Jake could accurately diagnose a nephew's Model T problems over the phone if the driver could describe the symptoms. As a teenager he built hot-rod racers for neighborhood kids using the Model T as a guide.

The Intercourse Stage

Beginning in the village of Intercourse, Coleman Diller drove a daily stagecoach through Bird-in-Hand and Smoke-

The last Lancaster-to-Intercourse stagecoach. It was operated by Coleman Diller and made a daily trip until 1910.

town to Lancaster until 1910. Two horses were hitched to the coach and the driver sat outside, up front. Sometimes one of the male passengers sat up front with him. The other passengers sat inside. Of course "Cole" hauled packages of all descriptions for folks enroute. He began his daily trip in the early forenoon and, upon arriving in Lancaster, usually stabled his horses at the Swan Hotel on the corner of South Queen and Vine Streets, directly opposite the Southern Market. If we wanted anything from town, Dad would telephone the appropriate store and have delivery made to the Swan before 1:30 P.M. Diller would then deliver to us on his way home to Intercourse in the late afternoon.

The Old Road, Route 340 today, was a dirt road from Intercourse to Bird-in-Hand. It was a cloud of dust in the summer and a sea of mud in the spring and fall until frozen in the winter. The stage had to go through regardless of weather. And according to accounts, there were many times when the Intercourse to Bird-in-Hand stretch needed four horses to pull the stagecoach because the mud was almost axle-deep at a number of places. When winter snows allowed sleighing, the trip was made by bobsled. The passengers sat in the open with more clothes than is customary today.

The Penn Highway Transit bus driven by John Burkey with its crash-type gear box and weak clutch. It replaced the Intercourse stagecoach.

As time went on, roads improved, and by 1910 a Lancaster-built Rowe Motor Truck was put into service by Mr. Diller. It was an historical event. Diller was the last of our old horse-drawn stagecoach drivers. When he sold his truck to John F. Burkey in 1917, he had served the community for about fifteen years.

Later, John Burkey added a bus service that included several daily Lancaster trips and served the White Horse area as well. Smoketown folks helped sponsor the service to get it going. In fact, Dad was one of the organizers.

The Penn Highway Transit Company was formed in 1923. The directors tried to sell stock to finance the venture. Because the stock didn't sell well, they offered books of tickets. People readily bought the ticket books, and the directors raised enough money to begin service. However, because people were using their previously-purchased tickets, there was little income. Also, costs were higher than expected.

Part of the problem was the design of the bus. Like all trucks and some early cars, the transmission was not synchronized. Shifting was not smooth or easy, and the driver

Tollgate and gatekeeper's house.

had to "row the thing through the gears" at every stop. That may explain why he often started out in second gear and "rode the clutch" to get going. Not surprisingly, clutch wear was serious, and expensive repair became necessary.

The Tollgate

The tollgate was a common ornament along all the "pikes" (turnpikes, toll roads) to Lancaster. There was one directly opposite the old Locust Grove School along Route 340 (now High Steel). A small house sat close to the road, and on the other side of the road a gate closed off one-half of the road. All folks driving past or through this gate had to stop and pay toll. The rate was seven cents.

In earlier days it was the custom for the tollkeeper to close the gate after bedtime, shutting off traffic. I don't believe this was done in my time. A tollgate was also located at Bridgeport, requiring another toll (this time 11 cents) just before crossing the narrow bridge over the Conestoga River. The last toll road I remember ran from New Holland to Lancaster, now Route 23. Local toll roads became impractical in the age of cars.

TRANSPORTATIONS IN THE EARLY 1900S

The Trolley

The electric trolley, or streetcar, was a popular way from here to there when horses were the main alternative. Trolley tracks ran to almost any main town along the pikes. The line from Lancaster to Coatesville along the Lincoln Highway was the most important for us. The trolley ran every hour during the working day and every half hour on Saturdays and several times on Sunday. Many stops were made along the way.

The trolley would easily get stuck in the snow. In January 1925 a trolley was stranded with passengers in the village of Lampeter for 36 hours. According to Lancaster newspapers, the people of Lampeter brought food to the stranded. The snow was too deep for the passengers to disembark. They were glad for the snowplow.

My brother Daniel and I would often shovel snow off the trolley car switches at the turnouts. This was frequently an all-night job. Much time was spent going from one place to another in the trolley boxcars. On January 3, 1925, we worked for the trolley company from 4:00 P.M. to 10:00 A.M. the following morning. We were paid 38 cents per hour, which came to a total of $6.75 with a meal included. That was real money.

The trolley was important to rural people. In my early years it was a real convenience, but by the mid-twenties it was being abandoned because of the automobile.

The Train

The main line Pennsylvania Railroad passed by our farm at Smoketown. When our cousins visited from Morgantown, they would insist that we go and sit along the bank to watch the trains go by. Every few minutes there would be a train, either a passenger train or freight with a long string of cars.

Because the locomotives used coal for fuel, sparks from the locomotives would sometimes cause grassfield fires along the railroad. When I was quite young, I remember getting up one morning and watching my brothers David and Daniel stamp out a fire in our grassfield. I remember Daniel

Hired man Aaron "Pete" Kennel at Witmer Station.

remarking that if they had not gotten the fire under control, God alone could have saved our buildings. There were no fire trucks until a later time. In addition to the many passenger trains, there was much freight for this was before the days of the long distance truck.

There were also many local trains during the day. Folks often checked their watches by the trains passing through every day at the same time.

At Witmer and Bird-in-Hand there were waiting rooms. Many trains stopped there in a day. The first train usually ran about 6 A.M. and was called the "News Express." Later trains stopped perhaps at 8 A.M. and 9:30 A.M. and again at noon and mid-afternoon and several times throughout the evening. People going to work in town and those on shopping tours made active use of the train. At the Witmer Station on both sides of the bridge facing westward, good wooden stairs were constructed so that folks could get to the train from either direction without crossing the tracks. Crossing the tracks was dangerous. Of course, folks walked to the station. A carefully laid flagstone walk, a community project, reached from the lower end of Smoketown (eastern side) to the Witmer station and on to the north end of Witmer. This was removed again in the first 50 years of my life when it seemed the need for this particular convenience had passed. In the mornings as we had breakfast we could see folks walking to "make their train."

The first steam train is said to have arrived in Lancaster on April 16, 1834. Horses had towed the locomotive from Philadelphia to Columbia. There it was checked and the boiler fired. It made the run from Columbia to Lancaster under its own power in just 55 minutes. Horses moved the Lancaster-Philadelphia trains.

Uncle John Beiler told us about the first steam engine train going east from Lancaster through Bird-in-Hand toward Ronks a few years after the Columbia-Lancaster train had converted from horse to steam power. "Some of us boys were out in the field sitting on the fence to watch it coming. When we saw the steam engine puffing, we got off the fence. We didn't want to be close to it if it should explode."

All the railroad cars were horse-drawn prior to this. The railroad track was flat iron about ¾ inch thick and about two inches wide supported on wooden beams. The wooden beams ran lengthwise so the area between the tracks was clear for the horses. Cross-ties and the "I" beam type rail came only after the railroads had converted to steam.

In the early days of under-powered locomotives with poor traction, there were problems on long grades. It was said an Amish family by the name of Diener had several boys with lots of energy who lived near the railroad. The track from Gordonville had some uphill grade. As a prank, the boys would sometimes take some of their mother's homemade soft soap and grease the track. Then they would hide nearby to watch the train stall. Finally it would back downgrade past the greased area. Then the engineer would wipe the rails clean and proceed with the train.

It was reported the trainmen were overheard grumbling that the urchins were probably watching nearby. Fortunately for them, they were not apprehended. Had they been caught, the trainmen might not have bothered sending them to juvenile court. Direct action and tender bottoms to remind them of the encounter seems more likely.

The Aeroplane

The first I recall seeing an "aeroplane" was on Friday, June 27, 1919, when three planes flew over us to Lancaster. There they made a loop and dropped some newspapers. In those days the sight of a plane was a special event. It was exciting.

The account of Lindbergh's flight across the ocean has always fascinated me. It was said that he took a lesson from observing the wild goose, which flies only when the wind is favorable. Reportedly, Lindbergh always packed his own parachute so that everything would be in order if he needed to jump. At the time, it did not occur to me that I would ever find flying commonplace, or that I would ever fly the ocean.

4.

Life and Work in the Early 1900s

Street Markets

The Lancaster street markets were important. Before the First World War, farmers would drive their covered market wagons to town, back up to the curb, and place a stand on the sidewalk to sell their produce. Supermarkets were far off in the future. Green vegetables were unknown in winter, and each market grower tried to have early fresh vegetables ahead of his neighbor in the springtime.

As I remember it, the street market extended along East King Street. But the advent of the car and the truck with fresh vegetables from the south changed the picture. Today the small truck farmer is nonexistent except for the roadside stands that seem like a resurrection of the pre-World War I curbside city markets.

"Truckers" (producers) would also take their produce to the market houses. Dad attended the Northern Market. At that time Lancaster also had the Southern, Western, East-

Lancaster's East King Street market at the courthouse steps. My parents took produce to this market in the early 1900s.

ern, and Central Markets. Many years later there was also a Fulton Market.

The market man would unhitch his horse and take it to the nearest livery stable. The Leopard Hotel stable where Dad parked his horse had two floors. A plank floor incline led to the second floor stable.

Trip to Philadelphia

Our family had a big, never-to-be-forgotten trip to Philadephia one day in 1911. On this particular day Dad and Mother decided to take us to see the big city of Philadelphia. Dad arranged to have a "through" train stop at Bird-in-Hand for his tribe and his cousin Annie Neuhauser. The people on the train who had wondered what dignitary was expected to board were no doubt surprised to see a lame Amishman and his wife get on with their four boys and two girls.

We visited Philadelphia and took a boat ride down the Delaware River on the ship *Brandywine* and returned on the boat *The City of Chester*. I remember how scared brother David was with the thought of going out on the water, but he survived the ordeal.

The zoo was the highlight among the places we visited in the big city. We lost little Jakie, but finally found him at the monkey cage; he was intently watching the monkeys.

We stopped at Bryn Mawr on the way home and visited a high-class Guernsey Farm because of Dad's interest in Guernsey cows. I recall that the owner of the farm, an aristocrat by the name of Miss Vaux, came to meet the train, again expecting a dignitary, probably because Dad wrote well and used his business letterhead. When the time came to leave, her farmer, Fred Hugler, a German immigrant, took us to meet the train in his old farm car, thus concluding the story without words. We came home to Bird-in-Hand the same day at about sundown. Ike Tshudy had the plant farm wagon and horse waiting for us. The plant wagon was a former covered-top market wagon with a shelf along both sides. The roof had been sawed off, so going home from the station we sat on the shelves. A good time was had by all. It was an adventure like few others.

School Years

I attended a newly built school in Smoketown. It was a two-story building with a basement. There were no indoor toilets, and water had to be carried from a neighbor's well and stored in an earthen container. Each scholar had his own drinking cup. These were all kept on a fairly high shelf. Sometimes mischievous boys would fill some of the cups with water. This was interesting for those who had to stretch to reach their cups. Imagine the surprise to find one's cup already filled.

I always loved school, especially the studying. Sports were not for me. At noon I would often run home for dinner rather than carry my lunch. I do remember one time I had my lunch in a paper bag, and only after I was nearly finished eating and found an orange did I realize I had another person's lunch. I was too ashamed to mention this to anyone. I also recall the teacher, Mr. Hunter, several times using the broom handle over the backs of some of the

The "new" school at Smoketown; razed and replaced by the consolidated school at the end of the Depression. That second school has also since been replaced, and the site now holds a beautiful new elementary school.

"difficult" older boys.

As far as school days are concerned, I always hated having to miss days. This was before the laws of compulsory attendance came along, so as soon as I was old enough to help, I was kept out many days, often to haul shipments of seed to the Bird-in-Hand freight station for the P.L. Rohrer Company. It was expected I would do manual labor as a vocation. My father considered education unnecessary for me. I didn't know one could be educated outside of school, but I read when I had the opportunity.

Mexican Crisis

Problems between Mexico and the United States in 1913-14 almost led to war. I well remember hearing a rumbling of thunder on a summer day in the west. One of Dad's workmen tried to make me believe the rumble came from the war in Mexico.

United States Marines and sailors had occupied Vera Cruz

to restore "order." Eighteen Americans were killed in the action, and many folks called for war with Mexico. But President Wilson would not yield to public pressure. His policy was called "Watchful Waiting."

The uprising was led by a bandit chief, hero if you were Mexican, named Pancho Villa. He led raids across the border into the United States. Since the Mexican government didn't deal with the problem, the president sent General Pershing with an order to go get Villa, dead or alive. The army couldn't find him. It seemed the next orders were, "Forget Villa." At least I remember a news cartoon to that effect.

1915 Pocket Money

It was during my late school years that I developed an interest in the adventure of trapping muskrats and skunks. Every morning during the winter trapping season, I would get up early and walk nearly a mile through the fields with a neighbor lad to the creek south of our home to check our traps. I think one season we caught 14 muskrats in as many mornings, plus a skunk.

I remember the reaction of the rest of the family sitting around the breakfast table the morning I caught the skunk. How they tried to hold their noses shut. I thought of it as a real achievement, because a skunk hide was worth about five dollars when a pair of shoes could be bought for two dollars or less, and a large cone of ice cream could be bought for a nickel and a small cone for a penny.

Filling the Icehouse

After I was out of school, at age 13, I was privileged to spend several winters in the home of Uncle Jacob R. Glick near Bard's Crossing. While there, I helped with the farm chores because their son Jonas was going to school.

Each winter we had to fill the icehouse cellar since there were no mechanical ice-making machines in use in the countryside at that time. We got the ice on the dam at Hunsicker's Mill. It was at least six inches thick. We sawed the ice with large tree saws. Of course, there were no chain saws then. We hauled these ice blocks several miles to Uncle Jake's farm on bobsleds and packed them in sawdust. The sawdust insulated the ice to prevent melting so there would be ice for the next summer.

In commercial ice-gathering ventures, special horse-drawn ice plows were used to cut nearly through the ice in two directions to mark it out into large blocks. The blocks were then easily dislodged and floated to the ramp where they were removed from the ponds.

In 1917 the ground froze soon after Thanksgiving. The weather stayed cold with snow cover until the end of March. For several winters when we had very cold weather, the roads would be blown full of snow. The snow had to be shoveled off the road by hand because there were no snowplows for rural roads.

Rural Electricity

Rural electricity came on the scene in the early part of the 20th century. Many small, local power companies sprouted. One power company near Leacock failed to get permission from a landowner to erect their poles along his farm. The farmer resented this and hired several young fellows, including an Amishman, to cut the poles down during the night. This resulted in a lawsuit. The Amish church elders also took a dim view of their member's uncharacteristic action and disciplined him for it.

Enos Zimmerman of Intercourse built his electric line as far west as Witmer to what is now Mt. Sidney Road. He operated as Intercourse Electric Company. As recently as 1932 when we moved to the farm where I still live, there was no electricity along Rockvale Road. This was a dirt road with grass growing in the middle as late as 1933. There were no stop signs along these roads. The driver to the right always had the right of way.

The Tinker's Contribution

The tinshop was an important place in 1910. The tinsmith's skills and services were a necessity before alumi-

51

num came along. Tinware served the everyday needs of families where aluminum and stainless steel now serve. Kettles, pans, buckets, dippers, and funnels were usually made of tin-coated iron sheet metal. The tinware would wear out. Repairing it kept the neighborhood tinsmith busy mending leaks and putting new bottoms into containers. America had not yet become a throwaway society. The tinsmith also made new items that were not yet mass-produced by factories. Most of the repairs were done by soldering. The invention of low-cost aluminum eliminated the need for a tinsmith.

Smoketown's tinsmith was an Amishman named Dan Beiler. An interesting character, he was an expert in his work, and he also knew how to tease growing boys. Perhaps he reaped what he sowed. In any case, life was never boring at Tinker Dan Beiler's tin shop. The tinsmith's older sister, Leah, kept house for him the first years he was in business. Apparently she had problems with cold feet at night. She would heat several bricks in the oven of their stove, wrap them in newspaper, and put them in the bed to keep her feet warm.

It happened that one night Leah accidently pushed these bricks out of bed. As they fell to the floor the noise awakened her brother. Partly in his sleep, he opened his bedroom window and took his gun and shot out the window to frighten the intruder away. Their neighbor, Mrs. Ben Myers, was up late doing some sewing. When she heard the gunshot, she decided there were thieves in the neighborhood so she quickly went to bed.

Tinker Dan was the target of pranks when the youngsters he had teased as children grew to be teenagers. Things that seemed funny to boys at the time would be hard to under-stand today. Now, for example, what youngster would think of relocating the flagstone sidewalk to the horse's hayrack in the barn behind the house? What village house now has a carriage and horse barn out back as a standard pattern? They are gone like the snows of long past winters.

Unfortunately, the tinsmith had a difference of opinion with his local bishop. That seems to be the reason he left

Smoketown and moved to Virginia. Perhaps he was restless, too. Later he moved to Georgia and then back to Virginia.

In 1970 he came back to Smoketown to visit. He stopped at my boyhood home, the plant farm in Smoketown, to see if he could find any of the Glicks. As it happened, my brother Jake's son, Jake Jr., and his family lived there by then. Jake Jr.'s children were playing in the yard, throwing water balloons at each other. Young Jeff threw a water-filled balloon at his sister who ducked to avoid it. As luck would have it, the tinsmith opened his car window just in time to be hit by the balloon. The horrified children ran away.

But Tinker Dan found someone who told him where to find my brother Jake. When he caught up with Jake, he asked if the young people now living in the old Glick home were another generation of Glicks. He didn't explain why he suspected as much.

5.

Farming Practices in the Early 1900s

Few things have changed as radically during my lifetime as the way farmers do their work. A rocket trip to the moon is hardly more astonishing than the advances I've witnessed in agricultural technology. Even in childhood, I remember we were already adopting modern methods as rapidly as possible. Sometimes we may have gotten a little too far out front when new ways were not yet fully developed.

Things had started to move a lot faster about the time of the Civil War in the mid-1800s. At least that's how my mother and her brothers explained it.

Mother's older brother was 16 during the summer of the Battle of Gettysburg (1864). On a visit with my son, he once took time to tell us about it. Uncle John and I were recalling World War I when my son observed that he (Uncle John) would remember the Spanish American War. John replied, "Oh, I remember the Civil War very well." Of course the conversation was in Pennsylvania Dutch, but translated it was about as follows:

"I was 16 years old. The wheat was ripe, ready to cradle. But many farmers were not harvesting. They said there was no use because the rebels were burning down all the barns as they came north. They were already in Maryland.

"My father [David Beiler II] said we would bring in the harvest, rebels or no rebels. I had to work away out in the hot sun, cutting wheat. It was hard, sweaty work, swinging the cradle from morning to evening. I would much rather have been sitting under a shade tree. But Father insisted. We cut the wheat.

"When we were barely finished, we got word that the covered bridge across the Susquehanna River at Wrightsville had been burned. The Rebel Army wouldn't be able to get across. Then, a few days later the rebels were turned back south at the Battle of Gettysburg. I was very glad our wheat was in the barn. Our neighbors who had expected the rebels to come burning had to go harvest their overripe wheat.

"Strange, the burning of a bridge could stop an army. Nowadays [1941] the lack of a bridge would hardly slow an army down."

Harvesting Wheat

At the time young Uncle John was cutting wheat, he used a grain cradle, a tool which was only in use for about 50 years. Before the grain cradle, harvesters had used sickles. The change from sickle to cradle boosted productivity. It marked the first significant change in method from the time of the biblical harvesting account found in the book of Ruth (2:1-3). But with a grain cradle, sheaves were still bound by hand with a twist of a few stalks of wheat. Binding was women's work. It was hard, stoop labor. All hands turned out to gather the harvest.

At harvest time, the grain was cut, bound, shocked, and hauled to the barn for storage. There was no time to thresh it then. "Thrashing" was a wintertime activity—after the corn harvest was finished.

While the McCormick reaper was a going thing by the end of the 1850s, none made it to Lancaster County until after the Civil War. When the reapers did arrive, they merely cut the grain, leaving it in loose "gavels" to be bound by hand by a crew of binders who followed the machine around the field.

The automatic twine-tying grain binder didn't make the scene until near the end of the 1870s when my father was a small child. One of the first twine-tying "self-binders" to come to Lancaster County was purchased by Joel Fisher, an Amishman who lived on the farm fronting Cherry Lane and the Lincoln Highway. The twine-tying self-binder was a revolution. One man, driving a team of horses, replaced a crew of a half-dozen people. The displaced binders grumbled, "How shall a poor person earn bread if they take away the work from us?"

After they were cut, the sheaves were set up in shocks to dry for a few days. A dozen or dozen-and-a-half sheaves were set up in a double row by hand. Then they were stored in the barn. Usually three or four horses were hitched to a "ladder" wagon with two men loading and two men pitching. The sheaves were carefully placed in perimeter layers; then the layers were tied together by the placement of sheaves in the middle layer. The grain sheaves were slippery, but with careful loading they would stay in place on the way to the barn, even over rough lanes. Loading a good, stable load that wouldn't slide off was an art now largely lost.

Once in the barn, the sheaves were unloaded into storage where they were again layered carefully. Men and boys with two-prong pitchforks threw the sheaves from one to another to fill the mow and the "overden" above the barn floor. As a 14-year-old, I used to try to catch the sheaves in mid-air and send them on to the next man without letting them fall. That saved some energy.

The man on whose farm I was working insisted I let the sheaf fall, then pick it up and throw it on. It never made sense to me then. Or now, either. I needed lots of reminding because I would soon be doing it the easy way again in spite of the objection.

Gathering the harvest required a crew. Usually it was a shared task with neighbors trading labor. Threshing, when

A locally-built pickup baler. This was a stationary baler with an engine and a cut-down hayloader used to pick up the straw.

we got around to it in the wintertime, also required a crew. It was dusty, hard, unpleasant work. I don't recall ever hearing anyone complain about the hard work, although my brother Dave used to object when chaff fell down his back inside his shirt.

It was hard work for the farm wives and daughters, too. They had to prepare the food to feed the hungry men. Large volumes of food were consumed. If the men worked hard, the women's tasks were no lighter. In fact, it may have been harder because the women had to look after the children and milk cows and feed chickens on threshing day, in addition to preparing food for crews of a dozen or more men. It took planning to have enough bread and pies baked ahead of time. Vegetable and meat preparation was more work then, too. It was not customary to buy ready-to-cook food at the grocery store.

The threshing crews went from farm to farm with the "rig." Sometimes they would sleep in the barn overnight, so the housewife might be feeding the hungry crew for three meals a day. It was not at all like inviting a group of people for a single social meal nowadays.

When steam power replaced mechanical horsepower to operate the thresher, the fireman had to arrive early to get

The Mennonite inventor of the New Holland baler, Ed Nolt (right), with a friend in 1989.

the boiler fired up for a head of steam by the time the crew arrived. He would need breakfast even if the others only came later.

Gradually, threshing became a summertime task as machine capacity increased. Now the memory of winter threshing has faded and the idea seems quaint. But the wheat was relatively safe from insects in storage in the sheaf. It would "go through a sweat" that helped it thresh out readily.

Today most cereal grain is harvested with a combine, and the straw is baled in the field. This only came about after a Mennonite inventor named Ed Nolt built a practical, automatic baler at the end of the 1930s. Nolt, who lived near Vogansville, Pennsylvania, had been a thresherman from the time he was 17. In 1936 he sold his rig and bought a combine, but farmers wouldn't let him cut their wheat because there was no good way to gather the straw. Loading the slippery straw like hay with a hayloader was a bust. The straw just slid off the wagon.

In 1940 Ed Nolt's baler went into volume production at the newly regrouped New Holland Machine Company under the leadership of J. Henry Fisher. Fisher grew up as our land-joining neighbor boy in Smoketown. The Fishers were good neighbors and the company J. Henry created was important to many people. They pushed farm technology far ahead in both hay and grain harvest.

Indeed, grain harvest came a long way in a single century. There were few if any threshing machines in 1800. Our Amish fathers and forefathers threshed grain with a flail. Sheaves were opened and spread out on the barn floor. The Quakers in Chester County are said to have used horses to tread out the grain. One had to be quick with a shovel to catch the horse droppings so they wouldn't contaminate the wheat.

One thing hasn't changed. The sight of a field of wheat shocks is still worthy of a painting. Except for the Old Order Amish and Old Order Mennonites, harvest rarely happens that way anymore.

By the time I was old enough to work in the harvest, steam power was standard. When the rig arrived at the farm, the thresher (called a separator in the midwest) was placed in the barn with a push-pole shoved by the steam engine. It would be blocked into place. A conveyor-like attachment called a carrier was projected out through the forebay door above the barnyard if a straw stack was to be built. Most farms had straw stacks.

Belting up the engine came next. Power was transmitted by a long belt to get the fire of the steamer as far away from the barn as feasible. The belt went from the engine flywheel to the thresher to supply power. Alignment had to be perfect; other-wise the belt would fly off the pulley. The engine driver had to be able to place his rig with great accuracy. He did this by sighting across the sides of the flywheel and the thresher drive pulley. It was a real art that few farmers today understand.

A few steamers had the flywheel on the side opposite the driver's position. That made sighting across the flywheel nearly impossible and complicated setting up to the belt. It has been suggested that the remarks of the operators would sometimes have produced a head of steam if they had been uttered into the steamer's firebox.

Straw stacks, once standard, are rarely seen now.

In any case, it was a hazardous job and accidents did happen. If the huge, long drive belt tore or ran off the pulley, anyone in the way would be seriously injured if not killed. More than a few men lost arms that way.

When everything was ready, the engineer would toot the steam whistle and threshing would begin. If the sheaves had been stored in the barn, a relay team of three or more would toss the sheaves to the machine. The "feeder" was careful to feed the monster very uniformly, overlapping each sheaf with the next, with all sheaves going in grain end first. Machine capacity could be maximized that way.

One or two men would be busy bagging out the clean grain. If the grain would be stored in bulk, it would be carried to the granary in bushel baskets. The straw would go out to the barn yard on the carrier. There two or three men built the stack, placing the straw with four-prong dung forks. The sheaf forks used for the unthreshed sheaves were two-prong affairs with short handles for use in the barn. For loading in the field, long-handled forks were used.

As I remember it, we built the straw stack by layering the straw much as one would layer-load loose hay on a wagon. A layer of straw was placed around the perimeter. Then more straw was trampled into place in what would become the center of the stack. When the stack was several feet high, the next layers were extended out a few inches to help shed the rain away from the base. From there the sides were angled in slightly with the center kept high to make it weatherproof. Layer by layer it grew, until it reached full height. At the end, the top was somewhat rounded to help it shed rain much like a thatched roof. Ordinarily, straw stacks were built only when inside storage was filled. Where in all of Pennsylvania could one find experienced straw-stack builders now?

Mowing out straw inside the straw mow was a very unpleasant task after blowers, or windstackers, replaced the carrier contraptions used earlier. To accomplish this task, the men worked in a choking cloud of dust. One would be spitting up the black dirt for days afterward. It was a job that would be given to the hired man and farmer's son or sons who couldn't quit and just walk away from it all. By lunchtime the fellows working in the straw would be black as coal miners at the end of a shift. But threshers were well paid. Because it was hard work, a man might expect $2.50 to $3.00 a day in addition to food.

In addition to other hazards, there was danger of fire. A spark from the steam engine might ride into the barn on the belt. Or a stray bit of wire could find its way into the machine or an internal part could come loose and strike a spark. The straw, chaff, and dust were almost explosively flammable. If a fire broke out, the steam engine operator yanked back on the throttle to stop the rig, gave a shrill warning toot on the whistle, and put his tractor into reverse. At the sound of the whistle, the men tossing the sheaves into the machine jumped to remove the wheel blocks and grabbed the tongue to steer. In a moment the machine would be dragged out of the barn which was often in flames by then. The machine might be damaged, but it would not be destroyed.

Make Hay While the Sun Shines

Hay-making changed little from the dawn of history until the 17th century. In the Old Testament time of King Solomon (Proverbs 27:25), grass was cut with a sickle and raked with wooden rakes. Scythes eventually replaced the sickle. The scythe was a major advance because a man could use the momentum and energy of his whole body to swing the blade. With the sickle he could only use the energy of one arm.

In ancient times the crop was native grass, not a planted legume. Seeded hay fields seem to be a more or less recent development. Ernest Correll, a German historian, reports that it was the Mennonite refugees coming out of Switzerland at the end of the Thirty Years War (1648) who made the change in Germany and France. In Switzerland these people had grazed cows in the highlands and cut wild meadow hay for winter feed. They milked cows and made butter and cheese. Apparently, they were dairymen, not grain farmers.

As refugees in the farming country of Alsace and the Palatinate they brought little but their skills and attitudes. Of the two, the attitudes may have been the more important. But apparently they wanted to keep on being dairymen, not farmers. That seems to be the reason they needed more hay than could be cut from swampy, untillable land. So they took the drastic action of planting cropland with hay. From somewhere one farmer found out about alfalfa and tried it. Another found clover. Correll thinks the clover may have come from the Dutch Mennonites who already seem to have understood the value of legumes.

In any case, something strange happened. When they discovered and planted legumes, their land became more productive. And the Mennonites, while scattered, got together for worship from time to time when they had the opportunity. When they did, they evidently talked about farming as well. So as soon as one knew something, they all seemed to know it. Thus they became well known in Europe as clover farmers.

According to Correll, their fame even threatened to get them into trouble. It seems some of their neighbors tried to have them driven out of the country on the basis of their obvious practice of black magic. "For their land is getting better when other people's land gets poorer." Obviously,

(top) We appreciated the dump rake for making hay. It was certainly easier than hand raking.

(bottom) Hand loading a wagon of hay involved coordinated communication, with the "loader" on the wagon shouting directions to the "pitchers," one on either side of the wagon.

those Mennonites must be in league with Satan. It didn't occur to the neighbors that the clover and alfalfa were responsible. Nitrogen was not discovered chemically until many years later.

Gradually the idea of crop rotations and seeded hay fields caught on. History records that by 1830, legumes, lime, and crop rotations were well accepted in Pennsylvania where many Alsatian Mennonites had moved. The combination kept Pennsylvania land fertile when other farmers, such as those in the southern United States, had exhausted their land, abandoned it, and moved on west. Be that as it may, clover, timothy, and alfalfa were standard rotation crops by the time I came along. We took them for granted.

When I was a boy, horse-drawn mowers had already been cutting hay for 50 or 60 years. Wooden hay rakes had been replaced by steel-tine dump rakes and side-delivery rakes were on the way. After the side-delivery rakes were in use, the dump rake stayed in use to clean up after the hayloader. Even into the 1930s we cross-raked our hay fields with a dump rake and found enough dropped hay for a windrow of "rakings" after we had loaded all the windrows.

Before the invention of mechanical hayloaders, the dump-raked hay would be gathered into heaps by hand using a fork. The hay cured further in the heaps which were some-times turned over. Each heap would make a large forkful of hay. When cured, it was pitched to the man on the wagon with long-handled three-prong forks. It was hard work for the three-man crew. For all that matter, it was work for the sweating horses, too. Horses would be in a shampoo-like lather of sweat and worried all the while by the stinging horse flies.

When I was a boy, one man on the wagon would load the hay pitched to him by the two men on the ground, one on either side of the wagon. They placed their forkfuls of hay according to the loader's direction. He would call out "layer, corner, middle, or binder" and the men on the ground would know exactly where to land their forkfuls, even if the top of the load was much higher than their heads and out of sight.

The practice was to start at one corner and go all the way around the edge of the wagon, overlapping each forkful. The last forkful on the outer layer was the "binder." Then the middle had to be placed to keep the outer layer in place so it wouldn't shift on the way to the barn. The middle had to be well tramped in. Layer by layer the load filled. At the barn it was pitched off by hand, a forkful at a time. Ordinarily the forkfuls coming off the wagon were the same units that had been pitched up from the ground in field. They stayed more or less intact until removed for feeding that winter.

The mechanical hayloader replaced the men with pitch-forks on the larger farms by about 1918 or 1920. The first such machines were reciprocating pushbar devices with forks that literally forked the hay up from the windrow. Chain and rope-slat conveyor machines came later. These in turn were replaced by the tight-bottom loaders that had a separate pickup but used pushbars to elevate the crop.

Unless there was a small boy available to drive, the horses were often guided by voice or a single line. If a small boy was around, he would be appointed to ride the lead horse for loading. Then if something didn't suit the men on the wagon, they would at least have someone to yell at. Sitting on the sweating horse wasn't all glory for a seven- or eight-year-old barefoot boy. The horse sweat would soak through his pants and give him something like a posion ivy rash from one bare ankle up and around and down to the other ankle. Guys who remember it also remember that they learned to walk kind of bowlegged. The boy would look forward to being old enough to drive from the wagon so he would not have to ride the horse. With the coming of the mechanical loader everything changed.

The practice then was to load the back half of the wagon halfway up, using the layered and trampled middle pattern as previously. Then the front of the wagon was loaded to the same height. Next the back end was loaded all the way up. Filling the front section completed the load. It all had to be done carefully to avoid an upset or slipping off on the way to the barn.

There were tiresome jokes. Those farmers with little formal education laughed at the so-called book farmers who had more education. One story that made the rounds told of a book farmer whose badly loaded wagon of hay had upset. To find out what to do next, he looked it up in the book. He discovered that, according to the book, he should reload.

Unloading at the barn changed when hayloaders replaced pitchers in the field. We used a two-prong spear or grapple. A man on the wagon would plunge the spear into the load and set the trigger. A rope running through a pulley near the peak of the roof lifted the hay to that point. The pulley was attached to a car on a track that ran across the barn from the barn floor to the haymow. When the spear hit the car, it released the car so it could travel across the haymow. When it was above the mow, the man on the wagon pulled on the light trip-rope attached to the spear so it would drop its load.

Power to pull the rope that lifted and carried the spearload of hay was provided by a horse in many cases. After 1937 we used our 1936 Ford car. The driver had to be careful not to back over the rope on the way back up the barn hill for the next grab. Otherwise, it worked well.

The hay had to be leveled out in the haymow as it was dropped by the spear or "hay hook" as we called it. It was hot and dusty work. But there was always a moment of relief. The falling spearload of hay would create a bit of breeze that was most welcome to the men mowing out the hay.

The hay would not be stored until it was thought dry enough for safe storage. But usually there was enough moisture remaining in the stems for it to "go through a sweat" and heat. Sometimes it would even steam, especially where the hay was dropped by the hay hook and compacted. Sometimes some salt would be scattered in the hope that it would help cure and preserve the hay. Frequently, charred pockets of hay were found the next winter, indicating a narrow escape from spontaneous combustion.

When hay was stored too green, it heated to the point of spontaneous combustion. Many barns burned as a result. If the problem was discovered in time, neighbors would gather and hurriedly haul the hot hay out into the field to save the barn. My brother Jake made a long hay thermometer with an iron pipe that could be inserted deep into the hay to discover if it was getting dangerously hot.

Haying was a once-a-year experience until the late 1920s. The hay was cut near the end of June, just before wheat harvest. The second growth was pastured. By then the permanent bluegrass pastures were less productive anyway, and the hay fields were a welcome supply of mid-summer pasture. This changed as more clover was replaced by alfalfa and dairymen discovered that hay cut at a younger, more immature stage would produce more milk. Now three or four cuttings of alfalfa per season are routine. With better fertilization, chemical insect control, and bud-stage cutting, the four cuttings produce nearly double the tonnage, and the hay may have twice the nutrient value on a per pound basis.

Hay crushers and crimpers came only after World War II. Experimental work with roll-type crushers dates from the late 1920s in California. A German patent was recorded in 1913, but the machines were not really practical and effective until well into the 1950s. Crops of today's yields probably could not have been cured before these machines became available. The haybine came in 1965 as a combination machine. Now most hay is harvested by these mower-conditioners of one sort or another.

Clover and timothy and alsike were the main hay crops when I was a boy. Dad used to mix a little alfalfa with the clover to inoculate the soil. Clover was sown with a hand-cranked spinner seeder attached to the bottom of a sack carrying the seed supply. The whole thing hung from one's neck. One walked across the wheat field in the late winter or early spring and scattered the seed for the hay crop for the following year. It would grow with the wheat and be back the next year as a thick stand of hay.

Fertilizing the Good Earth

Early in the 20th century it was customary for farmers to store all stable manure from their livestock in the *Misthof* (barnyard). The yard was enclosed with a stone wall high enough to keep the stock in. During the winter, there was a large accumulation of manure and straw which livestock were bedded down with daily. Sometimes a horse hitched to a heavy wrought-iron fork was used to drag the manure from the stable to the manure pile in the barnyard. The

67

manure was hauled out in the spring and spread over the fields. It was loaded by hand with a fork. This was usually a good spring job.

Since the cattle exercised over the manure pile daily, they trampled the manure and complicated removal. The farmer usually kept the accumulation of manure fairly even on top. Sometimes these large manure piles were covered with clean straw and used as a place to play cornerball at farm sales. The game would go on all day until the sale was over and it was time to go home and do chores.

The manure spreader came on the scene around 1910-1915. Prior to this, manure was loaded onto a flat wagon or cart and hauled to the field where it was knocked off the wagon into small piles. Later it was spread out with a manure fork by hand.

◆ ◆ ◆

Lime was needed to correct the acid level in soil when planting alfalfa. This was obtained by burning locally quarried limestone in lime kilns. Making lime was a trade of its own, but some farmers had lime kilns and manufactured lime when other farm work didn't interfere. After burning, the lime was distributed in the fields to "slake" and spread over the surface as evenly as possible. By the late 1920s or early 1930s, lime was spread mechanically by lime drills. Ground limestone replaced burnt lime about the time of World War II.

With the exception of landplaster (calcium sulphate) and guano from Peru, very little artificial fertilizer was used until after the Civil War. My dad's brother-in-law suggested Dad try some phosphate on his wheat soon after he was married. Dad tried it, saw that it paid, and was a steadfast believer in chemical fertilizer from that time on.

Corn Without Herbicides

When I was young, corn production was quite different than it is today. Hybrids were unknown, and variety improvement was mainly a matter of selection.

County Agent "Dutch" Bucher used to tell the story of a local farmer named Isaac Hershey who mixed several varieties to produce a cross he called Sure Crop around 1912. Hershey then selected the best ears from that first cross for seed in the following years. Bucher said it was years before the Hershey corn ears were sufficiently uniform to have an entry worth taking to the fair. But the corn proved superior in yield in good years and bad. Later it became one of the four "studhorse" varieties that most modern hybrids were bred from.

Like other open-pollinated corn, Sure Crop lacked stalk and root strength. Unless harvested as soon as the grain was about mature, the corn would "go down" and harvesting would be a mess. It frequently fell down even earlier if there was a moderate windstorm.

At silage harvest time when the stalks were still green and stiff, the corn was often too tangled for machine harvest. Farmers who owned corn binders often could not use them to harvest silage corn because the corn rarely stood well enough for binder harvest when the stalks were dry. Ordinarily, corn had to be cut by hand.

In my day, corn was planted at much lower plant populations per acre. When harvesting by hand, it was desirable to have large ears to reduce the husking time per bushel. With mechanical harvesters, the size of the ear no longer mattered, so farmers planted more seed per acre to increase the yield.

Corn also used to be planted in wider rows. Usually the rows were about 40 inches apart. Planting in 36-inch rows seemed like crowding it. The corn was "hilled," which meant that several grains of corn were planted in a group. Then there was a space nearly as large as the row width to the next hill. After the corn was up and growing, it was often hand-thinned to two or three stalks per hill.

Keeping the corn weed-free was a near impossibility in wet seasons and hard work even if the summer was dry. Cultivation and hand-hoeing were the only weed control methods available until after World War II when herbicides became available.

FARMING PRACTICES IN THE EARLY 1900S

Cultivation started soon after the corn was planted. Some farmers "blind cultivated" before the corn peeped through the surface to get a head start on any weeds that might already have sprouted. Others went over the field with a spike tooth harrow to tear out tiny weed seedlings just before the corn came up. Cultivation began soon after the corn spiked through. For the first time over, the cultivator was equipped with shields to avoid covering the small corn plants. Even so, one had to go very slowly. Young fellows sometimes fell asleep cultivating corn, especially on Mondays after an exciting weekend.

The next time through was easier because one could go much faster without covering the corn because it was six or eight inches tall. The third or final cultivation was done with disk hilling attachments on the cultivator to toss up a ridge of soil around the corn roots to bury any weeds on the row. From then to harvest time, the hoe was the only weed control remaining. Hoeing corn seemed to use up all available time for any available farm boys. Somehow, it made other recreation less necessary.

There was one method that worked better but required more time at planting. It was called checking. A wire with knots at the proper intervals would be stretched across the field and fastened to stakes at each end. Used with a checkrow planter, this wire would operate the planter shoe valves to drop the seed as the wire knots passed through the valve mechanism. With the corn in checkrows, one could cultivate the field crosswise as well as lengthwise and largely clear out weeds and grass. But planting was more complicated. The control wire had to be moved sideways as planting progressed across the field. The method is forgotten now. Few farmers under 50 years of age remember seeing corn planted in checkrows.

In August, when the corn was nearly mature, it was time to go through the fields and "make the bucks." A buck consisted of cornstalks from four hills being tied together at the top to support the shock that would be built around it a few weeks later.

Then, in September, the corn was shocked. Each person would cut the corn in one row for a space of six steps, carrying the stalks in his left arm and then setting them up around the buck to form the shock. The shock rows were six rows apart. Shocks were tied with tarred sisal twine we called tar ropes. The corn, both stalk and ear, cured out in the shock.

When the ears were dry, the shocks were broken apart and the ears husked out. A pile was made at each shock. The corn ears were gathered with a bushel basket and loaded onto a wagon. After hauling the load to a corncrib, scoop shovels were used to put the ears into the crib. Shovels were made of iron, not aluminum, and they were very heavy. Aluminum shovels only became available after World War II. The lighter shovels greatly reduced the effort needed to do this work.

The husked stalks were tied in large bundles and set up in large shocks in the field to dry further until they could be shredded and stored without danger of mold or spontaneous heating. Fodder shredding was wintertime work. The shredded stalks were useful for horse and mule feed and were used for bedding if straw was scarce.

The grain was ground if it was fed to cattle. For poultry and hogs, it was shelled. Most farms had a hand-cranked corn sheller. A large flywheel helped ease the task. The flywheel sort of stored energy between ears if the machine was cranked up to speed. A child could put the ears into the top of the sheller, but it took an older person to swing the crank. By the time the corn was shelled, the grain and cobs were very dry. The dry cobs were useful as fuel in the kitchen range, especially in summer when the housewife wanted a quick hot fire that would cook the food without heating up the kitchen.

That was one use we had for corn cobs—to start fires. I remember Mother once sent my sister Mary out to the barn for "*un par grutza*" (literally a pair of cobs, but meaning a few). Mary brought her just two. Then Mother explained that, yes, *un par* meant two if it was people. But in the case

Corn shocks were in style in the mid-1940s. That is me creating another shock.

of corn cobs it would mean a handful at minimum.

When hybrids with stronger stalks and roots came along, the corn binder suddenly became more useful and we stopped cutting corn by hand. The husker-shredder replaced hand-husking for some of us. Others husked by hand until the picker took over. That didn't happen until we had pickup balers and stalk shredders so we could save the stalks for bedding. Here in the east the picker did not replace hand-work until we had a satisfactory way to save the stalks. That all happened since the 1940s.

$195 and a FORD
make a guaranteed powerful
Staude Mak-a-Tractor
An advertisement for an early tractor.

Power on the Farm

Our farming was mostly done by "mule" power. All the plowing was done with a walking plow, where one followed the plow, holding onto two handles to guide the plow and walking in the furrow. When the plow point struck a rock, you were made aware very abruptly. I remember a time when the plow struck a rock and flew out of the furrow because of the fast-walking mules. The plow handles struck me in the ribs. I lost my breath for a few minutes. The mules, Rosie and Kate, soon learned to ease up when the plow came in contact with a rock.

The mules filled a real place on our farm. When we drove over the creek on the narrow wooden bridge without side rails they always pushed hard toward the middle, away from the sides. They seemed to have a fear of falling into the stream. In addition to the regular fieldwork, the mules and I made many trips to Dad's Honeybrook farm to haul supplies, a distance of over 20 miles.

This was the time when tractors were first coming on the scene for tillage, but were not too practical. Many were experimental models, almost homemade. Some were made with Model T Ford chassis. Others were huge, cumbersome things that seemed to descend from the steam tractors of an

Our 1927 two-speed John Deere "D" tractor with water injection carburetor. The radiator held a 100-lb. milk can of water.

earlier time. Dad purchased an Avery 5-10 tractor. It would do a fairly good job pulling a two-section spring harrow and roller. One time my brother Dan upset it doing grading work. Tractors were all on steel wheels. Rubber tires for farm implements were not introduced until the 1930s.

Sometime around 1920 we disposed of our small Avery tractor. In a deal with Kennel Brothers, Dad's cousins in Honeybrook, we bought a used Case two-plow tractor. The Kennels sold Ford cars and tractors. Soon after that, the Amish church agreed to limit tractor use to stationary power, not tillage. Brother Jake would use the Case tractor for disking on the sly, until Dad was told not to use the tractor in the field.

Dad hid the crank from brother Jake. There was no starter on a tractor in those days. So my brother started the tractor by cranking it with a pipe wrench. To Jake's disappointment, Dad finally insisted that Rosie and Kate, the mules, and the horse Lem, be used for fieldwork.

The early Fordson tractors would sometimes rear up on a

1930 cannery farm wheat harvest with Fordson tractor and binder.

heavy pull, flip over backwards, and kill their drivers. The drawbar was carried relatively high to transfer more weight to the rear driving wheels for maximum traction. This reduced front-end weight and increased the risk of back-flips. We asked "Shorty" Kennel, the dealer, if what we had heard was true. He said, "If any man stays on the tractor when he sees it coming up over he ought to be killed." Unfortunately, no one had reflexes to move out that quickly.

The flip-over propensity resulted in a new power farming system that came to use much later. In Europe, a man named Harry Ferguson designed a safety hitch for the Fordson and a coupled, but not mounted, plow that prevented the tractor from flipping over backward. The cost of the Ferguson patent didn't suit Henry Ford. Instead, he added fenders with a rear overhang that would catch on the ground to prevent the flip-over. The fenders had hip-pockets that were handy for carrying tools and hitch pins and the baling wire you'd need for field repairs.

Ferguson developed his safety hitch into the three-point linkage that's now standard on most modern tractors around the world.

An advertisement for an early International Harvester tractor.

6.

The Tomato Business and the Cannery Farm

My father's success was in part the result of his insight and careful management. But necessity also drove him to frugality. For example, when he wanted to do concrete work, he obtained cinders from the railroad company instead of the crushed rock that cost a lot more money. The cinders were free for the hauling, and his underage sons didn't need to be paid. I remember that the man who had the cement mixer and did our work accused Dad of using "railroad smoke" in lieu of gravel for concrete. But the so-called railroad smoke did the job for many, many years.

The Tomato Business

An interesting character came on the scene about 1914. His coming gave direction to many of us Glicks for the next forty years and even after World War II. A Philadelphia-area Quaker, his name was Hillborn. Mr. Hillborn came to the Witmer station by train and inquired for the Glick residence. One of us boys met him at the station. The others were at

Weaver's Feed Mill. He was quite anxious to see Dad, so we took him along in the market wagon pulled by our horse, Doll. On the way down he said, "Get up Doll, I want to talk to Mr. Glick as long as I can." This amused us. He wanted Dad to take over the tomato seed business he had developed, but Dad was a bit skeptical.

But Mr. Hillborn insisted, saying, "Mr. Glick, there's no string to this, I haven't come to sell thee anything, I give it to thee." In the following years our family and many others benefitted from his visit. "I give it to thee" became an honored phrase which is still often repeated among Glick family members.

Sometime earlier, my father had found an unusual redbeet with green leaves. It was a superior beet. He multiplied it and called it the New Century beet. It was under that name that he introduced it to the vegetable seed trade. Thanks to the beet, he became acquainted with the Philadelphia seedsman who sent Hillborn to Smoketown to find my father. Hillborn wanted to retire and turn his tomato-breeding business over to someone else. At that point, he was more concerned about finding someone who would value and continue his plant-breeding work than to merely obtain top dollar for his business.

He had started his business soon after the turn of the century. Mr. Hillborn spent his winters in Florida. There he grew tomatoes in the winter for the northern market. He was dissatisfied with the poor quality of the tomato varieties available and decided to do something about it.

By careful selection he was able to develop a globe-shaped tomato that would ripen up satisfactorily during shipping. He grew his own tomato seed in the north and sold it under seal. His seed was soon sought by other Florida growers. This was the tomato seed business entrusted to Dad with the words, "I haven't come to sell thee anything. I give it to thee." His gift was what is now called "goodwill" when a business is sold.

It was a milestone for our family and for the community and had a much wider influence in later years. It was fortunate that Dad decided to accept the responsibility to grow this special strain of tomato seed, the "Hillborn Selected Globe Tomato."

In later years Florida had a problem that almost wiped out winter-grown tomatoes. It was a disease called "nail-head rust." Our Globe tomato was then crossed with a French tomato, a variety known as Marvel, by the U.S. Department of Agriculture and called Marglobe. It was resistant to nail-head rust and still retained the Globe tomato shape and quality. It was soon joined by another cross developed at Rutgers University in New Jersey, which was named Rutgers in honor of that university.

Our Family Moves

The Smoketown years came to an end for our family when sister Malinda married Aaron Riehl on Thanksgiving Day, 1917. In the spring of 1918 the rest of us moved to what we called "the cannery farm" on Hobson Road. That is, we all moved except our dog, Sportie, who continued to go back to his former home to sleep (one mile away). Aaron Riehl would sometimes attach a message to his collar in the morning, since we didn't have telephones at that time.

Our neighbor Mrs. Laushey of the Laushey Nursery was said to have observed the change after 1918 when the Glick family moved out of Smoketown to the cannery farm. "It's so quiet, like a funeral," she supposedly said.

Before we moved to the cannery farm, it was tenanted by William Redcay who managed the tomato growing. The acreage of tomatoes grown in the first years was considerably smaller than in later years when the demand for the seed increased. During the first few years, a Greek food processing firm from Philadelphia—Coroneos Brothers—furnished the labor to pick and process the fruit. We took care of the seed and seed marketing. Coroneos Brothers usually hired recent immigrants, many of whom were Italians, to help us. They set up temporary housing in the small house at the south end of Buckwalter Road.

The tomato pulp was processed in the cannery building Dad

Our mules, Rosie and Kate, hitched to the spring wagon.

had provided. He also installed a boiler to provide steam for cooking the pulp. In the later years, he installed a much larger unit. During those first years, the pulp was put into wooden barrels for the Greek firm. After several years, it was packed in six-ounce cans which were steam-sterilized after packing.

Soon after we moved to the cannery farm, Dad decided it would be better if we picked the tomatoes ourselves. The connection with Coroneos Brothers was phased out. We started selling to Ransing Brothers Lancaster Vinegar Co. and hauled to their plant in Lancaster by tank truck.

In 1929 we installed the necessary equipment and began canning the pulp in No. 10 cans (nearly a gallon, six #10's = five gallons). We then started selling to Campbell Soup Company. Some of the pulp was wholesaled to Aument Brothers and the Rose Bowl in Lancaster. In those early years the tomatoes were hauled in from the field by our mules, Rosie and Kate, in our two-ton spring wagon.

At the cannery farm the tomato seed business had absolute priority. Preparations for planting were made during the winter months. Stable manure was composted. To make the compost, we would make a heap of manure about 50 feet long, approximately six feet wide and five feet high.

This entire pile had to be reforked by hand a number of times at about ten-day intervals. It was real physical therapy. There were no front-end loaders until almost 50 years later.

In the spring, the compost was mixed with water and a handful applied to the root of each tomato plant as it was set out. We planted by hand. In this we were following the instructions that came with the business from Mr. Hillborn.

At planting time, the rows were marked by shallow furrows and "checkered"; that is, marked out in both directions so each plant would be spaced at equal distance from the next. One tomato plant was dropped at each check. Then the handful of wet manure compost was dropped on the root. Next a half-circle of fertilizer was dropped around the root. The fourth person would cover this with soil using a hoe. The next morning the plants would be sitting up. It required a lot of work hours, but unless the cutworms interfered, there were practically no misses.

Dad soon experimented and found the use of a mechanical transplanter satisfactory, although not as accurate as the hand planting. It was much easier to cultivate both ways for weed control if the plants were checkered. The mechanical transplanting method saved a lot of time but required some hand hoeing during the growing season.

Many acres of tomatoes were grown under contract by other neighboring farmers. About 100 hundred acres were grown in 1936. That year the cannery turned out over 60,000 #10 cans of puree and two tons of seed. Each seed variety was kept carefully segregated to keep the lines genetically pure.

During the first years, the tomato pickers worked by the hour; the wages were 20 to 25 cents per hour. My brother David and I each had a field group to supervise. It was hot and some pickers had a tendency to pick very slowly because they were paid by the hour, not by the basket. There was also the temptation to throw tomatoes, especially if one thought the boss wouldn't see it.

Tomato picking was a backbreaking job for folks not used to stooping. In the early years the tomato pickers were mostly farm youth who were acquainted with farm work.

A wagonload of tomato pickers heading out to the tomato fields on the cannery farm along Hobson Road.

Many of them came from the Millwood, Maple Grove, and Peachey (now Weavertown) churches. Their association together became a social affair. In fact, a couple that first met during tomato-picking season was later married and lived, I trust, happily ever afterward. Amish youth from Iowa and Kansas also came to help in this seasonal job during the 1920s and early '30s. There were few off-the-farm work opportunities for farm youth then. Many of the Iowa and Kansas boys worked in the cannery. During the rush time of the season, some of them would work almost around the clock during the week. There was a certain competition to see who could put in the most hours in one day. One worker, who worked either in the cannery or on the truck that hauled tomatoes in from the fields, claimed to have worked 26 hours one day. The hours were almost that long and the work was strenuous.

The main truck driver, Jacob (Garver Jake) Stoltzfus, once went home from work very late. Unknown to him, his wife had cleaned house that day and rearranged the furniture in the bedroom. When he tried to get into bed in the dark without waking his wife, the bed wasn't where he expected it to be. It was reported that he landed on the floor.

In the 1920s a large steam boiler (150 HP) was installed

Tomato sorters "ham it up" for the camera.

in the cannery to provide steam to process the tomato pulp. The tomatoes were dumped into a washer tank. A conveyer belt moved them to the pulper where the rejects were sorted out by six to ten workers—usually girls. Then the entire tomato was put through the pulper. The seeds and skins were removed by the pulper. The pulp was pumped into wooden vats holding 500 gallons each. The two vats were then steam cooked to the desired thickness.

When ready to can, the tomato purée went into a steam-jacketed copper kettle holding 150 gallons until tapped out into the canner and canned in #10 cans, with an identification for each batch. The cans of pulp were sterilized and stacked in a large storage room until shipment.

Large leather mittens were worn to handle the hot, heavy cans. There were usually at least three men in "the bull pen," as the storage room was called. They would toss, catch, and stack the cans.

We had frequent government inspections to see that our product did not have a mold content. Bacteria were not a problem because of the steam sterilization. But a micro-

The cannery building on our Hobson Road farm which we called "the cannery farm."

scopic mold count would have shown if any low quality tomatoes had been included. The cans for every batch were stamped by number. If any tested defective, they would have been withdrawn. We had very few problems because our people worked carefully and removed below-standard fruit at the sorting table.

Some of the tomato juice was made into ketchup and sold locally. Also, some was canned and sold as a poultry food supplement. Tomato juice was recommended to keep the "poultry in the pink of condition," until the Post Office Department demanded proof of the claim and refused to accept on-farm experience and observation as evidence. The claim was dropped.

After separation from the pulp, the seed went into barrels with tomato juice and was left to ferment several days. Next, the seed was washed and dried in the sun, except during cloudy weather when belt-driven fans were used.

Boys and girls, youth and older people were pleased if they had work. There was also some city help. In later years tomato picking was paid by the basket. Field crew management suddenly became very easy. But labor became very scarce during World War II.

Near the end of World War II, we were assisted by German

prisoners-of-war from a stockade near Reading. That meant two 30-mile trips to the stockade every day. One of the Germans made the following comment about my brother Dan's son who was given the task of making the roundtrip drive. "*Der Isaak der fahrt wie ein Feuerwagon!*" (Isaac drives like a fire engine.)

✦ ✦ ✦

Following World War II, a group of local churches used the cannery to can food for relief for food-short areas in Europe. Supervised by Reuben Stoltzfus, it began in November, 1945. The final report profiles the effort:

Poultry, 20,509 chickens ....9,036 cans
Pork (300 hogs donated), 679 total....... 16,780 cans
Beef Paté (80 beefs donated), 311 total ..... 21,379 cans
Number of volunteer workers: 3,803; average per day, 50
Average cans per day: 1,264
Money donated: $153,549.00

Seventy-one congregations from eight Mennonite and Amish conferences were involved. They included Lancaster Mennonite Conference, Horning Mennonite, Wenger Mennonite, Ohio and Eastern Amish Mennonite, Old Order Amish, Weavertown Amish Mennonites, Brethren in Christ, and many others.

The use of the cannery for relief canning under Mennonite Central Committee sponsorship was a fitting climax to the tomato seed growing business. In Europe many starving war sufferers were fed. The tomato enterprise was slowly phased out due to post-war competitive reality.

The History of the Cannery Farm

The cannery farm where the tomato activity was headquartered was also known as the Hartman farm, because it was the ancestral home of the Hartman family who came from Switzerland before 1750. Dad purchased it about 1909. Located in East Lampeter Township, about five miles east of Lancaster along the Old Factory Road, now called Hobson Road, the farm land ends at what is now Elmwood

The 1754 Hartman house on the cannery farm.

Road. Elmwood Road was actually an extension of the farm
lane which Dad opened to the Old Philadelphia Pike.

The farm house was built in 1754. There was also a large
bank barn with tobacco shed and a corn barn. The soil was
sandy loam with limestone underlay. Mill Creek meandered
through the meadow. The pasture land south of the creek
is now Old Mill Stream Campground. Dad sold the farmland
south of the creek to neighbor Monroe Peifer but reserved a
right-of-way to the Lincoln Highway.

Mill Creek was important in the 1700s and 1800s and the
early part of the 20th century because it provided the water
power for at least ten flour mills within as many miles from the
farm. The mills have nearly all been abandoned. When the
western prairies were broken to grow wheat, Pennsylvania was
no longer wheat country. Instead it became dairy country.

The 1754 stone house on the cannery farm was in for a
face-lift when Dad took over. An older kitchen which may
have been the original settler's cabin on the north side was
torn down, and a new cement block kitchen with basement
was built south of the house in preparation for our move.

A tank was put in the loft of the new kitchen to store
rainwater from the roof. This water was circulated through
a waterfront in the kitchen range, providing hot water for
the kitchen.

There was also a cistern in the basement to store rainwater for washing. The basement got a walled-in iron kettle to heat laundry water. An entrance was built from the basement into the deep arch cellar under the main house.

When the well under the basement was being dug, the workers reportedly came to rock they couldn't dig through. It was said that Aaron E. Beiler crawled down into the well hole, placed the dynamite, and lit the fuse, scrambling out before the charge went off.

Adjacent to the basement was a woodshed with a coal bin and a built-in iron kettle used for butchering. The outside of the stone house was plastered over smoothly during our first year there. I helped to mix the mortar for the plastering job.

At the barn the stable was renovated. Hog pens and a pen for chickens were added in the west end. A large water tank had been placed in the northwest corner of the stable to keep it from freezing. Here rainwater from the barn roof was stored. Additional water was pumped from the well as needed. This water supply was for all outside needs, including cannery use. In later years a large cistern was made in brother Dan's barn to supply water for the cannery. An underground pipe was laid down the hill, below frost level, to the tomato cannery. The height of the cistern on the hilltop provided ample pressure by gravity. A well was drilled for additional water for the cannery.

I need to give credit to sister Mary, who had a lot of willingness and interest in getting the work done. In addition to helping with the house and garden work, she would whitewash the fenceposts around the buildings and the trees in the orchard north of the barn to the height of a fencepost. The lime mixture used for whitewashing lasted most of the summer. This gave the farmstead a neat and tidy appearance.

Our Guernsey Herd on the Cannery Farm

The purebred Guernsey young stock and dry cows were already stabled on the cannery farm prior to our move there and had been cared for by Dad's tenant, William Redcay, for a number of years. The herd consisted of approximately twelve milking cows—purebreds—in which our entire family shared a lively interest.

The cows were milked by hand, and the milk was put through a cream separator. We sent the cream to Lancaster by Trolley Express and sold it to an ice cream maker, Wertz & Co., at 20 cents a quart. The trolley station (Zook's station) was along U.S. 30 (the Lincoln Highway), just a few steps east of where Joe Myers Diner is today. We had about one-fifth of a mile from our barn to the trolley station. We crossed a wooden bridge over Mill Creek, went through a cow pasture, up the hill, and over a rock ledge. All with horse and wagon. The cream was shipped every other day.

The Cannery Farm Neighbors

Neighbors helped to make life interesting. Many a time we would rest our team at the end of the field to visit with our neighbors across the fence or across the creek. Neighbor Ben Denlinger to the east was a devoted Christian and a finicky farmer. He once commented about tractor farming, "That's not farming."

I especially remember one day when we helped him haul in his wheat sheaves from the field to store them in the barn until the threshing outfit came through to thresh his crop. It was a very sultry day. Later that night there was a heavy thunderstorm.

After we were in bed asleep, Dad called upstairs, "Boys, come quickly, there's a fire." Lightning had struck Ben Denlinger's barn and burned it to the ground. Ben was fortunate to have a steep hill on his farm—too steep for farming—on which were a lot of large trees ideal for the heavy timber needed to frame his new barn. The trees were cut down with two-man crosscut saws because chain saws had not yet come on the scene. From that experience I learned to saw without "riding" the saw. A local sawmill then moved in to cut the wood into lumber which could be used for framing a barn.

Finally the day for the barn raising came. The frame of the new barn was put together and raised by manpower with stockades—iron-tipped poles. I thought the boss carpenter was a bit loud. When they were pushing up the frame work, he would yell to the men, "As high as the trees." By evening a new barn stood where none had been in the morning. It was a satisfaction to the many neighbors who had donated their time and sweat to help make it possible.

Ben Denlinger's farm was later purchased and occupied by my brother Dan. Dan raised his family on that farm.

✦ ✦ ✦

Monroe Peifer, Jr. was our neighbor to the south along the Lincoln Highway where the Wax Museum is now located. He, too, was a devoted Christian, an unassuming person with whom one could feel at ease. We would sometimes visit with him for hours, sitting on opposite banks of Mill Creek, the boundary line between our two farms. He was a dairy farmer and in later years served on the mission field under Lancaster Mennonite Conference.

Monroe once told us a story about a city family passing by his farm at milking time who stopped to buy milk. On seeing the Peifers milk their cows, the people decided they didn't want any of that milk. They wanted the kind that came in bottles.

He also shared an experience he once had with another neighbor, Ben Mellinger. Mellinger was a cattle dealer, and he stopped by Monroe's farm to buy a cow. Mellinger tried to buy the animal much below market value, thinking Monroe wouldn't know better. Monroe pretended to be considering the offer but seemed to hesitate. Mellinger thought he was about to buy at his figure. He kept saying, "Come on, sell me this cow." But Monroe finally said, "No, I was offered more than that, much more." Mellinger was taken aback when he realized the sum that had been offered and gave Monroe more than the other offer.

Just across the Lincoln Highway from the Monroe Peifer farmstead, where the Myers Diner is now located, lived Monroe's father, "Old" Monroe Peifer. He was an old-school farmer. He had a deep concern for the welfare of others and was retired when I knew him.

THE TOMATO BUSINESS AND THE CANNERY FARM

✦ ✦ ✦

Just east of Old Monroe's on the hill was Zook's trolley station, since taken over by Host Farm. It was there that Johnny Zook lived. He was rather unusual in several ways. He had been Amish and seemed to be a kindly person, but he was not in fellowship with any church group for a number of years. In fact he had, as it was, his own congregation which consisted of only his immediate family—a son and three daughters.

It may be that he was a victim of circumstances. It is not quite clear what the problem really was, but there was a problem concerning an ordination in which it was said that he disagreed rather strongly with the ministers of his church. Because of the attitude he expressed he was excommunicated. His brother supported him. They worshiped together, just their two families, hoping and waiting for a reconciliation with the main group. When Johnny Zook proceeded to baptize his family without being ordained to the ministry, his brother Jonas Zook withdrew with his family and sought membership with a local congregation. Johnny's neighbor, Old Monroe Peifer, tried to help him seek a reconciliation with the Amish church, but to no avail.

Monroe once suggested to Johnny that he contribute something in clothing for relief that was being sent to South Russia through the Mennonite Central Committee at the end of World War I in 1918. He said, "No, it won't get there anyway." But he was finally persuaded. Quite a long time later, he was invited to go along to the Lancaster train station to meet the Mennonite refugees coming from Russia. Well, sure enough, when the people came off the train, one man was wearing an Amish frock coat with hooks and eyes. It was the coat that Zook had contributed for relief. Johnny Zook met his end in an accident when he got his arm caught in a drive belt from a line shaft.

My brother Jake and I sometimes caught pigeons in Johnny Zook's barn. Jake would shine a flashlight at the birds to blind them so I could crawl around in the rafters to their roosts and catch them. Next, I'd lock their wings and throw them down to the haymow to Jake. In the dark it didn't seem so scary. But in daylight the distance from the roof to the barn floor was frightening.

✦ ✦ ✦

Billy Walker, our neighbor to the north, was a unique character, too. One time the road by his house was blown nearly full of snow. Several of us were shoveling out the snow to get the road opened, and one of the group called in to Billy suggesting that he help us. He said, "No! I didn't put it there and I am not going to help take it away." And he didn't, either.

Frequently he came to our farm to get his gallon kerosene can filled from Dad's tank. He never paid for it, at least as far as I know. He would just say, "Charge it." This was the custom of many who bought at the local store at that time, but Dad wasn't keeping a book account like that. So one winter day Billy came to have his can filled while we boys were working in the tobacco stripping room where it was warm. Jokingly he said he wanted kerosene and not water, so he went along to see that the can was filled with kerosene. When he came back, he set the can outside the door and came in again to visit with us boys. Unknown to him, brother Jakie was outside and quickly emptied the oil into the tank and filled the can with water and set it down again as Billy was coming out the door to go home. He never suspected that an exchange had been made. Jakie said, "Oh, I was going to fill it with water, but I won't now." Billy said, "You'd better not." The next morning when his wife wanted to pour a bit of oil on some dry wood to start fire to make breakfast, there was ice on the inside of the can. "Oh, well," she said, "if we get it at Glicks, it's half water anyhow." She couldn't start her fire with that kerosene. It was a nasty trick. That ended the kerosene business from our farm. He never came back for more.

He did, however, fire our steam boiler at the tomato cannery, as well as do other jobs there. He was killed by a fast train at the Bird-in-Hand crossing.

✦ ✦ ✦

Our neighbor to the west, Billy Sprecher, was a victim of the flu epidemic in the fall of 1918. At that time many folks died from the flu. We even lost the local undertaker, Emil Veit.

✦ ✦ ✦

"Sellem, sellem, takem down and sellem," thundered Ben Mellinger as he began his public auction of livestock, cattle, and pigs. He usually bought for the low dollar. His excitement seemed to get the potential buyers into a buying mood. He usually had a lively auction.

Mellinger was our other neighbor to the north. He had three growing boys. They were full of life as normal schoolboys are. They wanted to learn how to say things in Pennsylvania Dutch, which their parents understood but didn't teach to their children. In our mischievous and thoughtless moments, my brother and I would teach them sentences using words which we were not permitted to say ourselves. We then made the young fellows believe the sentences meant harmless things such as, "Dad, come for dinner." We should have known better.

One of the boys, Jay, never really forgave me for the spanking he got as a result of his dialect language lesson. He thought he was calling his father to lunch, but they detoured by the woodshed.

The Mellinger boys had a BB gun, and they would sometimes shoot at their sheep. The sheep would jump because it would apparently sting a bit, even through the wool. They would soon get into the habit of jumping as soon as they heard a gun crack, even if they were not hit.

When we moved to the cannery farm, we would usually use the telephone at the Mellinger residence because we did not have our own.

I was often sent to move cattle for Ben Mellinger. Before trucks were plentiful, cattle were driven from farm to farm or to market on foot, even to the stockyards in Lancaster. Usually this involved two of us. I remember walking many a mile to chase several cows or heifers from the farm where

Ben Mellinger had purchased them to his sale barn at home. Most fields along the roads were fenced but we were at a disadvantage because the cattle could usually go faster on four legs than we could on two.

Sometimes the cattle were driven to the railroad. There were cattle pens at both Bird-in-Hand and Gordonville because cattle were often shipped to market by rail.

PART TWO:
THE ROARING '20s

7.

Life Among the Amish
in the
Early 1920s

Our Family's 1923 Transition

When I was growing up, our family was a member of the Old Order Amish church. As a young person, I attended the Old Order youth activities. It was customary to have a hymn sing on Sunday evening which was usually held at the home where worship services had been held in the morning. The singing was always in German. Singing hymns in English was not permitted at the Sunday evening singing. Other group activities included visiting at cousin get-togethers. This happened on the *zwischa* or "in-between" Sunday when we did not meet for worship. Worship services were held every two weeks. There was no Sunday school. Our cousins seemed to be well satisfied with the Amish status quo and were quite ready to express their opinions about those who differed. Our family, however, chafed a bit at the stringent regulations in the Amish church.

Dad was somewhat open-minded, and family discussions

concerning the situation had an effect on all of us. Even so, leaving the Old Order group was unthinkable. However, when my brother David lost his membership with the Old Order group because he decided to marry a member of the more liberal Peachy Amish Church, we came to reconsider our commitment. It was a dilemma.

According to the Old Order church discipline, we (the other members of David's family) were constrained like all other members of the church to keep the Bann. Based on such scriptures as "*Denn die Juden haben keine gemeinschaft mit den Samaritan*" (For the Jews had no dealings with the Samaritans—John 4:9), the ban required us to shun David and his family.

Our family agonized over the situation. Should the family also transfer its membership to the Amish Mennonite group which Dave had now joined? This would mean we, too, would be subject to the *Bann* and kept in the *Bann* for the rest of our lives by the Old Order group which included many of our relatives. The decision was painful.

It was especially painful because we had experienced the genuine love and care which is such a central part of Amish community life. Individually, Amish people are aware of personal worth and connectedness as members of the fellowship. As members of the church, we were connected with others in a sense of community. We were not alone in life's difficulties.

To understand this basic premise about Amish life makes most of the rest of Amish ways seem much less astonishing. People are Amish because they really want to be. That's the reason we accept the discipline and the special life styles. There is love even for those who leave the church. What is often called "shunning" by outsiders, who don't understand it, is really an act of love. It is also painful, as our family found out.

As ex-members we were not shunned in the sense that we were not spoken to. However, there were certain rituals of separation which we experienced. We understood that the purpose of those rituals was to win us back to the fellowship because we were loved. The church feels a keen sense of loss when any member leaves the fellowship and experiences joy when he or she is reinstated. Most Amish groups practice some form of shunning or excommunication. However, the Old Order Amish are the most rigid, excommunicating those who leave for reasons of spirituality, often joining groups which are similar to the Old Order Amish (which is what our family did).

We made the transfer to the Peachy Amish church in the fall of 1923. At that time, the Peachy group was not much different from the Old Order church. Like the Old Order group, the church held worship services in homes on alternating Sundays. There was no Sunday school, and we also used the German language in our services. However, we did not place those in the *Bann* who sought membership with other groups of similar faith. When we transferred our membership, the Peachy Amish church was still quite new.

Following an 1877 division among the Amish in Lancaster County, two distinct groups had emerged. The church-house Amish met in meetinghouses and were not as conservative in thought and life as those who came to be called Old Order Amish. Between 1877 and the early 1900s Old Order people could freely join the church-house group without being disciplined. For example, "White" Amos Stoltzfus, later a minister at Millwood (one of the church-house groups), had been a member of the Old Order group. His girlfriend was a member of the church-house group. When they decided to marry, the Old Order gave Amos a membership transfer letter for the church-house group without placing him in the *Bann.*

However, White Amos transferred his membership before the so-called Moses Hartz controversy. Moses Hartz and his wife were excommunicated by the Old Order Amish for refusing to shun a son who had joined a local Mennonite church. Because a church-house Amish group received the Hartz family as members, refusing to recognize the *Bann,* the Old Order Amish churches became much more strict and began imposing the *Bann* on anyone who left the church, including those who joined church-house Amish groups.

Because some members of the Old Order Amish church (such as our family) disagreed with this position, they left the Old Order in 1909 and formed the Peachy Amish church. This division was a result of the *Bann* imposed between the churches. It was not, as is commonly reported, because of any desire to accept the telephone or other technological innovations. In fact, during the early years telephones were not permitted among the newly formed Peachy Amish group.

When we became members of the Peachy Amish church, we found the youth group included some members of the Old Order, as well as the youth of the Peachy group with whom we felt comfortable. We greatly appreciated the use of English hymnbooks at the hymn sings of the new group.

These hymn sings were often held on Saturday evenings, as well as on Sunday evenings. I remember one time we had a hymn sing at our home. There were also some Maple Grove youth (one of the church-house groups) there. There was continual singing from eight o'clock until midnight.

The singing schools that were held at the local Mennonite churches by David Wenger were also valuable instruction for our group. Some of the Maple Grove youth would also sometimes attend these youth activities. There was not a great difference in dress or life style between the church-house Amish and our group.

Weddings Among the Amish in the 1920s

Weddings were occasions of joy. For the Amish, weddings, like funerals, were community events. November and early December was the traditional wedding season. By then the most pressing farm harvest work was finished. Tuesdays and Thursdays were great days. That's because Mondays and Wednesdays were needed for preparation because there might be 200 to 400 guests for several meals in the all-day-and-evening event. An invitation was a cherished honor, especially if you were a teenager. Usually a teenager would only be invited as a cousin of the bride or groom.

Uncles and aunts were invited. And generally, the fellow

members of the church district. The wedding ceremony took place in the home of the bride. If he came from another church district, the groom might also invite his close friends if the home was large enough to accommodate the additional people.

The date was held as a close secret until announced at the end of the worship service on a Sunday preceding the wedding. The announcement usually came as a genuine surprise to most people.

However, within the family, preparations were also made long beforehand. For example, additional chickens or other poultry were often raised because roast chicken was the main feature of the wedding noon meal. Entire tubsful of bleached celery were needed in addition to the vegetables, so the garden planning was well thought out far in advance of need.

Most of the food was prepared the day before the cere-mony. Relatives and close friends considered it an honor to gather to help. The bride's parents directed the work, but they did no work on the day of the ceremony. Part of the preparation consisted of removing furniture from the main rooms downstairs and placing enough backless benches to seat all the guests.

The seats were filled by 8:30 in the morning when the service began. Hymns and preaching continued until noon. There were always two hymns sung from the *Ausbund*, the oldest Protestant hymnal in continuous use anywhere. Singing was in German in very slow tunes resembling Gregorian chants. The second hymn in the wedding service was always *"O, Gott Vater"* (Oh God Our Father). This hymn predates the Reformation and still is, for me, one of the most deeply moving worship hymns ever written. As the Old Order Amish sing it, it takes twenty minutes to sing the four verses.

A sermon followed the hymn singing. Then the entire congregation knelt for silent prayer, rose, and remained stand-ing while the deacon slowly read a chapter of the Bible. By the end of the reading, it was a relief to sit down again, even on a backless bench. The main sermon followed. This was preached by the bishop who united the couple in marriage. By then the clock on the wall was usually nearing 12:00 noon.

The marriage ceremony was patterned on the account from the book of Tobias *(Apocrypha)*, chapter 7, verse 15. Before pronouncing them man and wife, the bishop asked the couple if they promised to be faithful to each other until death ("*Bis der Todt Euch scheide*"). Divorce did not occur in Amish society.

After pronouncing the couple man and wife, the bishop was seated. He then called on visiting ministers and honored older relatives of the bride and groom to give testimony. These responses amounted to short sermons in their own right, with scripture quotations and good wishes for the newlyweds. The well-wishing usually included a ritual wish for "*ein guter anfang, ein standhaftes mittle aus zuharre bis ein seliges end.*" It was a very emotional time for the participants, even though many in the congregation were preoccupied by stiff backs by the time the elders finished sharing their lengthy thoughts.

At that point the bishop again asked the congregation to kneel, as he led them in a long, audible prayer. When the congregation rose, the benediction was pronounced, another hymn was sung, and the ceremony was completed.

Then the entire group left the room so that some of the benches could be raised on trestles and converted to tables that lined the walls, extending through double doorways into the next room to a corner and into the other direction. The corner was the place of honor and was occupied by the bride and groom. The tables were set quickly and the first seating took place. People went to the table to eat, not to visit. It would be insensitive to linger since other guests were outside waiting for their meal in a later seating. The tables usually seated 70 or more couples per seating. Friends and relatives of the newlyweds served the table. Serving was considered a special honor.

The food was wonderful. At noon there was always roast fowl with very rich filling, gravy, mashed potatoes, cooked vegetables, relishes, crisp celery, cakes, pies, and other desserts. There would be another feast in the evening. Most of the afternoon and evening was spent singing old German hymns that had been part of the Amish tradition for centuries.

Coming of Age in the 1920s

I was 20 years old when our family switched church affiliation in 1923. By then, World War I was over.

In the Ukraine, flour milling and farm machinery industries were largely in the hands of the Mennonite colonists whose ancestors had fled from the Low Countries. Many first went to Poland; then migrated to Russia at the invitation of Czarina Catherine, a German princess. By the mid 1920s, the Russian Revolution had disrupted and destroyed most of the progress of an entire generation. Famine followed. The American Mennonite reaction to that led to a major relief effort which eventually became Mennonite Central Committee.

In 1919, future president Herbert Hoover was named head of the huge international relief effort to feed the hungry in Europe. His success is one of the few things that came out of World War I which Americans can look back on and feel good about.

8.

Everyday Life in the 1920s

Traincar Loads of Fruit

"*Wir hon zvo leichte die woch.*" (We are having two funerals this week.) This was the introduction my parents received as they met one of the families on their visit to Croghan, New York, in August 1921. Dad often repeated the incident to us because he found the difference in dialect interesting. In Pennsylvania German, we said, "*Miah hen zweh leichte die woch.*"

Dad and Mother and Mr. and Mrs. Jonas Stoltzfus had spent several days in Ocean Grove, New Jersey, on vacation. Leaving Lancaster on August 8, they went to Ocean Grove and then went up the Hudson River past the Palisades to Watertown, New York. There they visited the Conservative Amish Mennonite folks for perhaps a week.

While he was there, Dad was able to locate a carload of peaches and have them shipped to Bird-in-Hand by railroad. They also bought a barrel of maple syrup and included it

103

with the car of peaches. The peach crop in Lancaster County that year had been a failure because of the late spring freeze at blossom time. So the peaches were appreciated.

The carload of peaches was scheduled to arrive at Bird-in-Hand on a certain day. Dad had cards mailed to the local rural route box holders and also distributed to various market stands in Lancaster City. People began arriving for peaches before the car came in, and Dad was swamped with customers. Being in real need of help, he saw a man walking along the road rather briskly. He asked him to help sell peaches. Isaac Garrett was a complete stranger, but Dad sent him out with a horse and spring wagon load of peaches to sell to the rural housewives.

The other workers laughed at Dad's move. They said, "You will find your horse tied to the fence and the man gone with the money." But he returned and had sold a lot of peaches. In fact, Garrett worked for Dad later. Today it would seem too risky to place similar confidence in an unknown stranger.

The barrel of maple syrup included with the car of peaches from New York was rolled out of the railroad car, loaded onto a spring wagon, taken down to Jonas Stoltzfuses (across from Bird-in-Hand Hotel), and rolled off into their front yard. Unknown to them, the syrup had fermented en route. Jonas Stoltzfus sat on the barrel, astraddle like on a horse. When he knocked the bung out of the barrel, the fermented syrup shot up, geyser-like, all over his face and beard. His wife said she never knew she had such a sweet husband.

The year after his experience with the carload of peaches from New York, Dad bought a carload of apples from Delaware for us boys to sell in the city of Lancaster. We were sent to peddle from house to house. To truck fruit was not feasible at that time because of the jolting damage caused by the solid tires on the trucks. One of the apples was a new variety named Nero. I remember one housewife exclaimed, "Nero! Nearer My God to Thee," enjoying her pun. Well, we sold the apples. My share of the profit was 50 dollars.

It seemed that Dad was always afraid that his sons would run out of work. So he started lots of projects and taught us that we must never run out of work in all the days of our lives. We used to envy other boys who could lie around on rainy days because we always had work to do. Dad believed in Proverbs 22:6.

The Griest-Musser Political Battle

Our local senator was a man named Griest and his opponent was a man named Musser. Musser had been a cattle dealer before being elected mayor of Lancaster. Now with Griest up for reelection, the opposition sponsored Musser. The local debate heated up beyond any in memory. Even among the nonpolitical Amish. Griest understood what now are called constituent services, but Musser was thought a more capable, if not more honorable, man. Griest was reelected, and a building on the square in Lancaster was eventually named for him.

Shortly before the election, there was a corn husking at the Mose Beiler farm on Musser School Road. Normally, a husking was a deal where the host benefitted from work done in exchange for the food he would serve afterwards. That didn't happen on this occasion. The Amish teenagers, all too young to vote, started arguing the Griest/Musser question and stopped husking corn to argue. Several got carried away with it all.

"Sandy" Christ Stoltzfus (for Musser) and Sam Fisher (for Griest) were coming to blows, but were separated before there was a serious fight. A fodder shock was burned, for which the Musser faction was blamed. Not a usual corn husking at all. The young folks were so preoccupied with politics they even forgot to look for a red corn ear which would have entitled some lucky young man to kiss a pretty girl. A pity.

Gone Fishing

One very warm Sunday afternoon in July, part of the youth group came to our home. The girls decided to go wading in Mill Creek in our meadow. When they returned, my sister Mary said that the fish swam against their legs. We boys questioned this, so we decided to investigate. When we got to the creek, we found the water very low because the millers upstream had closed their dams' watergates to accumulate water to run their mill machinery the following week.

Ordinarily, when we went into the creeks to swim, we would use a rail from the fence under our arms for flotation while we were learning to swim. We used the rails in the same way the next generation used inner tubes. Everyone always had his bathing suit on underneath his clothes. On this particular day the water was so low we didn't need a rail for flotation. As we were lounging about in the water and in the shade, one of the boys reached under a rock and came out with a big fish. Soon others did the same. This was exciting. We had perhaps a dozen or more fairly good-sized fish lying on the bank when someone reminded us that "today is Sunday," and one doesn't fish on Sunday. For a bit we were in a dilemma. It seemed a waste to throw the fish back into the creek. Then someone came up with an idea. Why not put the fish in Glicks' walled spring until a later date? Then we could go fishing when it was "legal" to fish. We quickly sent brother Jake to the barn for a gunny-sack feed bag.

Sometime later the fellows went fishing at Glicks one evening. Their parents were amused when they announced their intention. They were greatly surprised when they came home with large fish. The carp we caught lost their muddy flavor after being in clean spring water several weeks. This was of course explained to our parents later. Now there's a real fish story!

A Visitor from Germany

"Das hat Mir meine Freiheit gegeben." (That got me out of jail.) Old Heinrich Shultz, an itinerant German, stayed at our farm several weeks during the winter when I was in my late teens. Today he would be called a homeless person. At the time most people called him a tramp. If a wanderer, he

was not without dignity. I remember he once showed us a piece of tree bark with which he was able to play tunes by taking it into his mouth, something like a flute.

He had a warm place to stay with us in the stripping room of the tobacco shed. This work room was heated with a small coal stove for the winter task of preparing the tobacco crop for market. The coziness and warmth made it inviting in cold weather. Shultz was pleased to bed down there. It was much more pleasant than any place in town for the homeless. And Mother's food was better, too.

He made his own kind of contribution by being himself. We learned some High German from him. Indignantly, he told us all about how he had been jailed in Maryland for having spoken his mind. "*Ich wahr in Maryland, in die peach country. Sie haben mich denn Kaiser geheisen, das wollt Ich nicht Leiden. Ich habe sie meiner Meining gesagt das der kaiser ein guter Mann sei. Dann haben sie mich in die jail gethan. Dort habe Ich ihnen 'Maryland, My Maryland' geblasen. Das hat Mir meine Frieheit gegeben.*" (I was in Maryland in the peach country. Some of the people spoke evil of the Kaiser, and I could not stand it. I gave them a piece of my mind, and said the Kaiser was a good man. They put me in jail. While there, I played the song "Maryland, My Maryland" for them. This gave me my freedom.)

Shultz told us the marshal came to him after hearing him play and said, "I did not want to arrest you. You may go if you promise you will not speak your mind anymore."

"*Dann habe Ich gesagt* (Then I said), I thought this was a free country. I did not know it was wrong to speak your mind."

But the marshal said, "This country is at war; you are not free to speak your mind." What the marshal apparently did not know was that the Maryland song was really the tune to the old German folk song, "*O, Tannenbaum.*"

✦ ✦ ✦

It was at the start of Prohibition that Shultz visited us. As a German, he had difficulty understanding a country that would give up beer and make wine and schnapps illegal. He

Ball team. Front row, Jacob Augsberger, Christ Beiler, Christ Kauffman, Elam Beiler, and John Kauffman. Rear, I was umpire. Ben Lapp, Elam Kauffman, Emanuel Lapp, John B. Lapp and Brother Jake, our catcher.

thought of a way to compensate. His idea was to open a place of business where people could get together and sing and drink hard cider.

He would call the establishment "Shultz's Apfelwein-garten." We explained that hard apple cider, as an alcoholic beverage, would be illegal, too. He found this a real disappointment. "*Ich habe geglaubt das dies frei waehre wie die Milch.*" (I thought cider would be free of legal restraint, like milk.) Ultimately, Dad arranged lodging for Heinrich Shultz at the County Home. That was the last we heard of him.

Play Ball

Our Peachy Amish youth group often gathered to play baseball on holidays and sometimes on Saturday afternoons. There were no evening games. Farm work lasted until sundown, and the slow horse and buggy travel didn't allow time for evening games. The church frowned on Sunday ball playing.

However, it was a nice summer day. Dad and Mother were in Iowa visiting with friends. Brother Jacob and I had been at the Maple Grove Church the previous Sunday. We had visited friends in the afternoon and played ball a while in a crude way, using a pick handle, or something like that, for a bat. I'm not certain about any gloves.

We invited our friends to come to our place the following Sunday, suggesting we might play ball a while. We didn't have in mind a large social affair. Somehow word got around that the entire youth group was going to Glicks on Sunday. The Millwood and Maple Grove churches were one congregation at that time. Many of the members were also our relatives. In fact we knew each other rather well.

Come they did. It was said that some of them even skipped Sunday school; many skipped church services. The crowd was going to Glicks to play ball. That was not exactly what we had in mind.

They came for lunch. Sister Mary was swamped with dinner guests. Of course, Mother had canned vegetables and meat she could heat, but the fresh sliced peaches were all gone quickly. When several complained, Mary opened jars of canned peaches. Thanks to her, no one went hungry. They came to play ball and how they played. Even some of the girls batted. What a day!

The minister at Millwood couldn't understand why the youth weren't in worship services that morning until someone said the youth group had gone to Glicks. That afternoon as the Millwood deacon, Isaac Kennel, was on his way to visit his wife in the Lancaster Hospital, he went west on Route 30. Driving by, he could see the crowd of youth in Glicks' field on the north side of the highway. That told the tale. He was surprised that Dad Glicks would allow ball playing on Sunday. He later learned that they were out of state.

The entire happening was not quite what we had planned. We were embarrassed and still are. A little. In 1990, a Sunday baseball game hardly seems sinful. Attitudes change.

Horses I've Known

When I was young, it was the custom for sons to work for their parents until age 21. If any worked away from home during those years, they would usually be allowed to keep some of their wages. However, those who worked at home were seldom paid wages.

During the later teen years, young men usually received a complete driving outfit, beginning with a harness, then a buggy, and later a horse.

In the 1920s, horses usually provided the power for most of our transportation needs. Dad had a farm in Honeybrook, and I made many trips between our home farm and the Honeybrook farm. I drove two mules hitched to a large spring wagon of about two tons capacity to deliver supplies and to bring feed back for our smaller farm needs at home. It was a three-hour drive one way. I often made the trip in the evening, stayed over with the farm family, and returned the following day.

We had several horses that deserve mention. One was Doll, a good work mare, but prone to an unfortunate mania for running away at times. When I was just a lad, I once drove Doll east through Smoketown when she decided to take off. I was frightened, but I managed to head her into the side of the blacksmith shop which stopped her. She wasn't always so easy to stop.

Then there was Maud. Old Maud, we called her. She gave us six or seven colts. One, named Rex, probably had to endure too much teasing from us boys. He would snap at the person feeding him. Old Maud was a good driving horse. Once when she was left to find her own way into the stable, it happened that little Jakie was playing under the forebay just outside the stable door. Maud carefully stepped around him.

On another occasion Jakie and I were riding Maud up the road. She went a bit too fast for comfort. We had no saddle and I was afraid she would cause us to fall off, so I insisted that Jake shouldn't hold onto me so tightly. I even gave him a couple of punches, but he, terrified, held on to me all the more tightly. Somehow we got to our destination safely.

Once Dad and brother Dan drove to Honeybrook with our horse Bronco hitched to a light wagon. Bronco had a reputation: a mind of his own. When he decided he had gone far enough for a while, he would stage his own sit-down strike. He didn't really sit down, he just refused to go any further. Most of the time I could get along with him and keep him going, but this time Dad and Dan started off, and everything seemed to be going well until they started up the mountain at Beartown. There Bronco decided to balk. I think Dad tried all he had ever learned in reasoning with horses, except to build a fire under him.

It is said that someone had once done this, but to their consternation the horse went forward only a few steps, leaving the wagon over the fire. The horse still would not budge. That was Dad's problem with Bronco that day on the Beartown Hill. Finally a housewife who lived beside the road ventured out with a suggestion, "Mister, maybe his collar is too tight."

"No," Dad said, "the problem is farther up than the collar." Exasperated, Dad was in no mood for advice. The trouble was in the horse's head. I often think of this when dealing with people. Many times the attitude toward an issue is more obstacle than the issue itself.

Then there was my horse Sparky. He was almost as tough as leather and knew a few tricks. For instance, before Lancaster installed traffic lights, traffic at the busier street corners was regulated by patrolmen during rush hours. They used hand operated stop-go signals. Once I was driving Sparky east on Chestnut Street at the intersection of North Queen Street long before either became one-way streets. I was signalled to stop, as traffic was moving north on Queen Street. By merely pulling on the reins I could get Sparky to rear up on his hind feet. Sparky and I did our little act. The patrolman quickly stopped the northbound traffic and signalled for Sparky and me to go on. In the years since, I've sometimes wished for a similarly easy way to change red lights to green at my convenience.

One evening during early fall, Dad drove Sparky to Bird-in-Hand to Uncle Jake Beilers. Jake was our mother's brother. Sparky was tied to the hitching post until late in the evening, perhaps longer than he thought necessary. I think he was cold. Finally Dad got ready to go, and what he didn't know was that Sparky was in a hurry to get home, and even a bit irritated about his long wait.

Sparky decided to take Dad home in a hurry, but Dad objected. When he tried to slow the horse down, Sparky indicated his displeasure by kicking. Dad saw he needed to let him have his own way about it and they went faster and faster. Dad was terrified and not a little miffed.

Finally Dad had a ray of hope. By now he was near Smoketown where he saw a covered market wagon ahead, and by steering Sparky directly into the rear of that wagon he was able to get him into neutral gear and stopped. He put Sparky in brother Dave's barn in Smoketown and walked home the rest of the way. The walk was more than a mile, quite a distance for a man with an artificial leg.

The next morning Dad wanted to buy Sparky to shoot him, but I refused to sell him, feeling that, after all, Sparky was not fully to blame for what had happened. I'm sure Sparky didn't mean ill by it all; I knew him too well to accept the idea of ill will on his part. Dad and the horse just didn't understand each other.

Horse travel also involved other things. We didn't need to go to the garage for repairs or a tune-up. But we went to the blacksmith to have the iron horseshoes replaced from time to time. This was a real event when I was a youngster. The blacksmith had a fire in his forge to heat the shoes. When they were red hot, he would bend them to the desired size on the anvil to fit the horse's foot. In warm weather, we always had to keep the flies chased off the horse during the shoeing so the horse wouldn't kick the smith. We chased the flies with the tail of some dead horse; it made a fine switch. That's what live horses use tails for, too.

The saddler or harness repair man was also very impor-tant before automobiles took over. Our harness repair work was done by a man with one leg named Ben Schaeffer who lived in Witmer. Grandfather Glick, who was also a saddler, had taught him his trade.

9.

Sisters
and
Brothers

Malinda was my half sister, the daughter of Dad's first wife. She was enough older that she seemed like a grownup to me when I was a toddler. She helped our mother raise the rest of us. For her, our mother was her mother, too. She was born in March of 1896 and lost her mother only a few days later, so she had no recollection of her own mother at all. That kind of tragedy was not at all unusual before the discovery of antibiotics and the development of other modern medicine. Childbearing was hazardous. In the western world, at least, it's hard for today's generation to grasp the health hardships endured by their great-grandmothers.

Malinda married Aaron Riehl on Thanksgiving Day in 1917 when I was 13. I was living at the Honeybrook farm, helping Joel Stoltzfus at the time, but I remember having the day off to go home for the wedding. Malinda and Aaron are both gone now, but their very gentle, talented children and grandchildren are evidence of the heritage of that home.

Aaron and Malinda Riehl. Malinda was my half sister, the only child of my father's first wife.

✦ ✦ ✦

Dave was the oldest brother. And possibly the gentlest. His sensitivity to the aspirations and inhibitions of others was an overriding characteristic. It would have been very painful for him to think that he had somehow offended or embarrassed another person. We lost him over 50 years ago in 1936, and the loss is very real, even yet. His wife Barb was left with six young children. In spite of the difficult circumstances of the Depression she kept the family together, ran the farm, and raised the children. As children and adults, they have been a credit to both their parents.

David was perhaps a bit more reserved and quiet than the rest of us. I well remember the good counsel he gave his younger brothers. In some ways one might say he was Dad's right arm in the farm work for he had already been given the responsibility of overseeing the farm management in his teen years at Smoketown.

It was usually a problem to get us boys out of bed promptly in the morning. David was able to stump on the floor with one foot while the rest of him remained in bed. So it would sound downstairs like someone was getting up if Mother had called upstairs, "Feet on floor." Sometimes Mother would ask Dad to go and get us up. When we heard him coming up the stairs dragging his artificial leg, we usually got up quickly. Sometimes one of us would sneak down and imitate Dad's steps on the stairs. It usually worked.

Brother David seriously objected to his sleeping companion, who was usually brother Daniel, touching him. So one night Dan got out of bed and with either his cold toe or hand touched David's back. David tried to hit him, but hit the bed rail instead. Another time, soon after this, Dan accidently brushed against him, and this time David hit his target!

Dave managed the fieldwork. In those days farming was all done with horses, a walking plow, a spring harrow, and a roller. For sowing cabbage seed in the field, a drag was used to make a level seed bed. The cabbage seed was sown with a hand-pushed single row drill. After the plants were through the ground an inch, they needed to be cultivated with a wheel hoe, also pushed by man power. This was before the days of steam seedbed sterilization or chemical weed control. Brother Dave made sure all this work was done.

He was also always ready to help others. When Nick Capp was in jail, Dave came to his rescue and stored all his old cars. Nick was an Italian immigrant and an interesting character. He had gotten into difficulty with the telephone operators whom we called "hello girls." When they were bored and not busy, the operaters called him to hear his comical, broken immigrant English. He would lose both patience and temper and use language that the telephone company objected to. This was before the introduction of the dial telephone. To call someone you had to ring the operator and give the number you wanted. The operator

My oldest brother, Dave, with his dog, Tippy.

would connect you to your party and ring for you.

After he swore at the the operators repeatedly, the telephone company sent three men to remove his phone. He locked his door. He claimed they broke his door, to which he took large exception. One phone company employee was clobbered. When the other men ran, Nick grabbed his shotgun. He knew which man had broken down his door. His ire was directed at him especially. Actually, at the man's rear end.

Dave cultivating corn with Rosie and Kate.

He later said, "Me feel sorry for him? He make all the trouble. I grab the shotgun and shoot him mit shot." Apparently, too many pellets lodged in the phone man's rear end, so they put Nick in jail. He said, "They putta me in college." This was when brother David came to his rescue and took care of his things and stored his cars at the Baker lime-kiln property north of Witmer, which Dave had rented at the time.

Nick dealt in scrap iron. When the ten-inch iron pipe water line under the abandoned railroad bed at the north of the Smoketown farm became available, Nick dug up the pipes and lifted them out of the ditch with a tripod and chain hoist manned by several workers who had strong backs. I remember that I helped load the pipe, but I don't remember if I was paid. I remember that I quickly discovered that it was easier if I could get the longer end of the bar when two of us were lifting a heavy cast-iron pipe by passing a bar beneath it. The trick of shifting an unequal share of the weight onto your partner became known as the "Nick Capp holt" among ourselves. There were no ditch digging back-hoes or front-end loaders in those days.

In later years when brother David farmed at the southeast corner of Routes 896 and 340 in Smoketown, he had a small dairy with a milk delivery route along 340 in Smoketown and Bird-in-Hand. This was before mechanical cooling. He would bottle the evening milk and lower it into his deep well for cooling overnight for early morning delivery. By the time the hired hand had the morning milk cooled and bottled, he would already be back from early delivery. His dog Minkey would always be at the driveway waiting for him, watching in the direction he had gone.

Folks who had difficulty meeting their milk payments were given the opportunity to help him on the farm as payment. If the family had problems, he just forgave the bill.

He was always interested in new things, like electrical farm equipment. When an early version of the Ford-Ferguson tractor with hydraulic lift was demonstrated in 1936, he and brother Jake went to see it. He made sure his younger brothers got the know-how he had learned on his own.

Brother David was also interested in the differences in the Amish and Mennonite church regulations on dress and life style in the various areas. When several Russian Mennonite refugees came here after World War I, one had a mustache. Dave wanted to know if they were required to grow a mus-tache by their church in the manner that the Amish required a beard. The man was somewhat bewildered. He replied, "*Nein das ist wie man will*" (No, this was as one chooses). Brother David died October 3, 1936.

✦ ✦ ✦

At home, brother Daniel usually could think of interesting things to do as a teenager. I recall once the neighbor's bull came to pay a social visit to our cows and came up to the barn with them for some supper. Daniel thought it would be a good idea to tie a tin pail to his tail and send him home. When we left him out of the stable with the pail tied to his tail, he hesitated at first, but soon got started out hurriedly and seemed to gain momentum as he was going down the cattle lane toward the pasture with the pail swatting his legs as he ran. When he hopped over the first gate, all we could see were his rear legs and tail with the pail dangling in the air. He crossed the wooden bridge over Mill Creek, and when he came to the gate at the other side of the pasture, he hopped over the gate, leaving the bucket behind.

I don't remember this bull ever coming back to visit our cows again. At the time, it would not have occurred to us that there was any cruelty involved. Perhaps we should have been ashamed.

My brother Daniel's most important work of over 90 years may have been his involvement in the Christian Day School movement in Lancaster County. In fact, it's fair to say he was the father of this movement among the Mennonites in Pennsylvania. The first Amish or Mennonite school in the 20th century was at Greenwood, Delaware. But in 1939 the Locust Grove School opened its doors as an alternative to the consolidated public schools. To a substantial extent it was the result of Dan's effort and organizational skill. At first, many parents were dubious, but in the course of time there was a large positive response.

Those typing lessons that Daniel took during recess time from the sixth grade upward when he was in grade school helped make possible a work of which eternity will reveal the results. In the beginning, he merely handled correspondence for the family business. His horizons widened with experience and years. Ultimately, his leadership ability was recognized, thanks to his unselfish service. "For such a time as this" (Esther 4:14). At 93 years of age, brother Daniel continues as secretary emeritus of the Locust Grove Christian School Association. He invested untold time and energy in the effort. It might have succeeded without him, but it would not have happened then or there.

Lillian, Dan's wife, was an extraordinary person. Creative, talented, and supportive, she made their home a place of hospitality and peace for her children, her guests, and

My brother, Dan, and his wife, Lillian, shortly after their marriage.

strangers. There was no question at all about her native artistic ability. Food, as she served it, was not only delicious but very attractive. Her house was organized in the same manner. She didn't have more expensive things than other Amish women, but she somehow managed to make the house seem exceptionally attractive with an atmosphere of calm and peace. She was a very gracious person and undoubtedly accounted for many of her husband's and her children's accomplishments.

Dan, as noted, was the business person. He lived on a

small farm but usually spent his time in the office, not on the farm. His support of the family business was probably more important than our father would have conceded. In any case, both were insightful, independent thinkers. Very independent thinkers.

◆ ◆ ◆

Jacob was my younger brother. He has been a blessing to me for over 80 years. He was always considerate in spite of the embarrassments I must have caused him. Like our mother, he has always been kind. I can't recall he ever raised his voice with me. As the youngest son, he spent more time with his saintly mother than the rest of us. It may have helped mold his character. I remember when we played on the floor with our homemade toys. We each had a ship; mine was the Royal George; his ship was the Royal Chester.

As a young child, Jacob already had lots of self-confidence. He was sure he was able to do things without assistance. "*Ich kann selvert*" (I can do it myself), he would say, even when he needed help.

I was not always as kind as my little brother in our play. I recall that one time I told him, "Do you know that you are not really one of the family?" How I could think anything so cruel, I don't know. He didn't believe me, so I said, "You have light hair and blue eyes, and the rest of the family is dark complected." I continued, "One time a neighbor woman brought you here when she brought some old clothes and we kept you." Brokenhearted, he went to Mother. Mother laughed and said, "*Er set schlaeg hava*" (He deserves a whipping).

Another time brother Jake hit me on the back of the head with a small stone or dirt clod. Of course, I ran and told Mother. She called Jakie in to give an account of himself. He said he just wanted to throw it out into the field but his hand slipped. Mother said, "You must be more careful." That's the way it's always been with wise mothers and young sons. Ultimately, we both grew up.

Brother Jake was Dad's main support in the greenhouse business for all things mechanical or electrical. He seemed

My younger brother, Jake, and his wife, Katie, in 1992.

to have been born with pliers in hand. He had the ingenuity and push to get things done, even the seemingly impossible. Instinctively, he would see what the problem might be and go right to the solution.

I remember that Dad acquired a small two-cycle engine along with some other junk. Brother Jake, as a young teenager, got that engine to run by tinkering with it. He didn't always know just why things would work, but he had the satisfaction that they did work. Brother Jake was also the main force that kept the cannery machinery going, as well as the personnel. When Dad died in 1946, the tomato canning came to an abrupt end because Jake had to leave to take over the Glick Plant Farm at Smoketown.

As chief of the Witmer Fire Company, he found opportunity to put his talent to work in a way that benefitted the entire community. He mounted a 1000-gallon tank on a truck to haul water to neighbors who were out of water, and, not surprisingly, the local volunteer fire companies were soon using the tank for fire fighting. The tank was always loaded with water. Witmer Fire Company installed a two-

My sister, Mary (right), with a friend.

way radio in the truck to make it a more effective extension of their fire fighting effort. The radio made it possible to get in touch with the truckload of water on its way to a customer and divert it to a fire as soon as the call was received. The service is now operated by his son, Melvin, as Glick's Water Service.

From the time we lost brother Jakie at the zoo and found him watching the monkeys, he has always had an inquisitive mind that he used for the benefit of everybody without thought of remuneration. That continues. He invested untold days and hours in the establishment of the Tel Hai retirement home. He was also one of the main supporters of the Mennonite Central Committee relief cannery which was started when the Glick cannery was closed.

Jake and Katie's children had the good fortune of growing up in a home that was far less stressful than most because of the thoughtfulness of both their parents.

Like the majority of Amish women, Katie's artistic talents were channeled in the direction of domestic art, especially food and needlework. Her grandchildren are not alone in

My sister, Mary, entertaining our little sister, Dorothy, on their bicycle.

treasuring the large number of superb quilts Katie has produced since her family is grown and gone.

✦ ✦ ✦

Sister Mary took an active part in our family life until the family circle disbanded after our mother's death. Mary had been homemaker for Dad, Mother, Jacob, and me during the latter years of Mother's illness and the year following Mother's death. In the early months of 1927, Dad remarried to Leah Zook and moved to a house at the end of the cannery farm lane along Hobson Road. This was where sister Dorothy, now Mrs. Roland Yoder, was born.

One of my childhood memories involves Jakie and Mary. Jakie demonstrated how one could defy gravity by swinging part of a bucket of water back and forth until he could swing it up and around over his head without spilling a drop. He didn't tell Mary about the critical item of speed and centrifugal force. So she got wet when she tried the trick. I'm not sure what she did to him for that.

My half sister, Dorothy, with her husband, Roland Yoder, on their wedding day.

Mary was a treasured sister, but it was hard not to tease her when we were growing up. She had worse problems with our bees than we did. Once she decided to take some honey out of the hive, insisting that she wasn't afraid of them. So without bee smoker or bee regalia, she proceeded to take the hive apart and take the honey out. It wasn't the best. The bees were so angry that they swarmed over her and covered her legs. In desperation she ran to the horse water trough and plunged into it to get rid of the bees. Sadder, but wiser.

The extended Glick family at Christmas, 1936. That's Jake's family on the left; he's holding Johnnie. Melvin, Edna, and Norman stand in front of their parents. Anna and I (without a hat) are next. She is holding Jay Elvin. Ivan stands to Anna's right, between her and Jake's family. Our little Ada Marie has her broken arm in a sling. Gathered next to us is Dan's family. Dan isn't in the picture because he took it. Dan's wife, Lillian, stands between her daughter, Ruth, and Dave and Barb's daughter, Mary. Gathered in front of Ruth are Dan's other children—Ike, Vernon, and little Orpha. Dave is not in the picture because he died earlier that year. Dave's Mary and Elsie and their mother, Barb, are next with Lena, Elma, Daniel, and little Elmer in the foreground. The Riehls are next. That's Elma between Aaron (with hat and glasses) and Malinda. Rebecca (standing directly behind Malinda), Mary, and Sadie (holding Lois) are next with Aquilla and Evan in front. Dad is next with his fourth wife, Mabel, and little Dorothy. Sister Mary is on the right.

Later Mary worked as a maid in a Jewish home in Reading and spent a year in California. She returned to become active in Dad's greenhouse business in Smoketown.

Dad had a cottage built for her next to the present Turkey Hill Minit Market. It was a charming, compact dwelling. Here she had independence and the opportunity to entertain her friends. In her latter years, she operated it as a guest-house called "Aunt Mary's Cottage" until someone appropriated her sign. She continued the effort until her last illness. She lived very simply because it pleased her to be able to give the profit from her guesthouse venture to the Lord's mission work.

Mary invested 40 years of her life in mission effort at the South Christian Street Mennonite Church in Lancaster City's Seventh Ward. She taught a community Bible class, had a tract ministry, and also taught a girls' club basic cooking class for many years. It gave her joy to observe the pleasure and self-satisfaction the girls achieved as they learned to cook and prepare delicious food. She made the young girls aware that they mattered and that she loved them. In the process the girls were made aware of their own worth. She didn't have to tell them that she loved them. They knew it.

During a period of racial strife that flared up in that part of Lancaster in the 1960s, sister Mary was the only white person who could enter the Seventh Ward alone any time, day or night, without fear of being accosted. It seemed that everyone in the Ward knew "Miss Mary" and returned the respect they knew she had for them. Eternity will reveal the results of her ministry. She died in 1981 in her 80th year.

✦ ✦ ✦

Dorothy, my half sister, was the daughter of Leah Zook, Dad's third wife. She was born after I had left home, and I never learned to know her well. In fact, Dad had more than a dozen grandchildren before she was born so she grew up as one of the cousins, not as their aunt. In creativity and competence she is very much the daughter of her father. A nurse, she also became active in social work and combines the skills to help older people to richer, more fulfilling lives. Her husband, Roland Yoder, is a teacher and gifted artist.

There were two other Glick children. My little sister Annie died as a child in 1910 at age five. John Lewis, Dorothy's full brother, died in 1933 at the age of one year and three months.

10.

Pleasure in the 1920s

Train Excursions

On August 20, 1921 an excursion train to Atlantic City, New Jersey, left Lancaster at 7 A.M., arriving in Atlantic City at 10 A.M. Chriss Kauffman, Abner Stoltzfus, brother Jacob, and I went on the excursion. It cost $7 each. We returned to Lancaster at 9:30 P.M. that same day.

There were no gambling casinos in Atlantic City in those days. Going to the shore meant enjoying the water and sand and gathering shells. It was good fun and different from swimming in the creeks at home. Men's bathing suits were not yet topless. Sometimes the suits we used in the creeks had neither tops nor bottoms.

✦ ✦ ✦

On December 24, 1921, Jonas Lantz and I went to Belleville by train. We visited friends there over Sunday and came home on Monday, December 29. We walked all the way from Belleville to Reedsville for the train, a distance of about 10 miles. We had dinner at Lewistown and stopped over at Harrisburg to see the capitol building on the way home.

✦ ✦ ✦

In the 1920s, it was not unusual for some of the young fellows of our local churches to go west during the summer to work on farms. They usually traveled by rail. The first stop would often be in the Kalona, Iowa, community, after which they would move on to Kansas to work in the wheat harvest. Wheat farmers on the Plains were still using binders or headers to cut their grain, as the combine had not yet replaced those systems.

After the Kansas wheat harvest, the men would often go on to Colorado Springs and the Pikes Peak area for a vacation. Next they traveled to North Dakota, often by way of Yellowstone Park. Since the Dakotas were further north, wheat in the Dakotas was planted there in the spring, not the fall, and ripened later in the season.

These itinerants worked on farms along the way to earn money to keep going. But by mid-summer one fellow had to write home for money, saying that he was "not broke but badly bent."

My brother Daniel and his friend, John Blank, decided to "go west" in 1923. John Blank wanted to surprise a friend, Thomas Miller of Kalona, Iowa, whom he had never met but with whom he had been a pen pal for a number of years. Miller planned the same thing at the same time, so they passed each other en route without knowing it. Needless to say, both were surprised.

✦ ✦ ✦

It was a custom for Amish groups in each locality to extend hospitality to visiting youth groups from other Amish communities in the winter time. Whenever a group from another community arrived (usually by train), this would include a social gathering every evening in a different home. There were parties with lots of game playing. During the daytime, the group would visit in different homes. In this way the young people of widely separated communities learned to know each other.

It was also not unusual for young fellows from other communities west of Pennsylvania to find employment in the Lancaster area, sometimes for several years. Often they worked in the building trades. In December of 1923, I accompanied August Wicky, one of these young men, on his way home to Michigan. We went by train and made a few stops with Amish groups along the way, including a visit in Belleville with Minister Sam Peachy and Bishop John Zook. It is to these men that the Peachy Amish church was indebted for ministerial help at its beginnings in 1910. That's the reason the congregation was called the Peachy church. In later years when the church became part of a wider fellowship of churches it became known as a Beachy church.

We continued by train from Belleville and the Big Valley by way of the Horseshoe Curve, changing trains in Pittsburgh. We spent time in Hartville, Ohio; LaGrange, Indiana; the Wicky home in Michigan; Allen County, Indiana; Adams County, Indiana; and Kalona, Iowa.

While in Kalona, Iowa, I met Anna, the girl the Lord had chosen to become my companion for more than 50 years. She had the keen insight and capability that one rarely finds.

I stayed in Iowa nearly a fortnight during a mid-winter thaw. The mud roads were so sticky that the mud would stick to the spokes of the buggy and fill up between the spokes. There were very few gravel roads in rural Iowa in 1924. One could go faster by walking than by horse and buggy. Sometimes we walked on the edge of the field when the horse had all he could pull just dragging the empty buggy through the mud. Cars didn't have a chance.

I left Iowa by train from the Kalona station on Monday evening, February 4, 1924. I spent several weeks in the Holmes County, Ohio, area visiting with people like the ministers Sol Slabach and Rob Troyer whom Dad had

(top)   A Montana homesteader's residence.   Sister Mary and I visited relatives in Montana in 1925.

(bottom) Ezra and Lydia Borntrager and family in Montana, 1925. Lydia Borntrager was my dad's half sister.

learned to know through business. I was royally entertained. The experience was a milestone in my life.

Revival Meetings

Revival meetings in the local Mennonite churches were a time of spiritual refreshing for us. There was an element of adventure because the Amish church did not practice this Methodist innovation. We attended meetings at Mellinger's Church in November of 1924 held by John W. Weaver of Union Grove and at Millwood Church by David Garber from Ohio.

Meetings were also held at the Monterey Church of the Brethren. The weekend Bible instruction meetings held occasionally at the local churches, featuring some of the best Bible teachers of the day, were also something I looked forward to. I am sorry to say that this practice has long since been discontinued.

The year 1924 came to an end with usual youth activities. We had the privilege of attending Bible conferences, both at Millwood Church in November and at Morgantown in December. This was the beginning of the Saturday afternoon German school that prepared the way for Sunday school for our Peachy Amish church later.

Sister Mary and I Head West

During the summer of 1925, sister Mary and I visited our relatives in eastern Montana, stopping to visit other friends in the midwest. We included some sightseeing, traveling by train with a round-trip ticket.

We left Lancaster on the morning of July 9 and were able to see the Horseshoe Curve on the Pennsylvania Railroad line. That evening we arrived in Nappanee for the stopover in Indiana. We had changed trains several times. My special friend, Anna Glick, was in Indiana at the time and met us at the depot. She also arranged weekend lodging for us while we visited friends in the community.

We got to Bloomfield, Montana, on Wednesday, July 15. While there we visited with our Grandpa Glick's sons and

(top) Uncle Henry Glick, a 1910 Montana homesteader, loading wheat sheaves.

(bottom) Montana range horses coralled for spring farm work.

daughter by his second wife—Uncle Chriss, Uncle Henry, and Aunt Lydia (Mrs. Ezra Borntrager). This part of the Glick family had homesteaded land near Bloomfield in 1910 and 1912. When we were there in 1925, the farm work was being done by branded wild horses that lived on the range most of the year. The jack rabbits were plentiful, and coyotes howled in the night. We visited our uncles, the several cousins, and a few other Amish folks who lived in the area. One of them remarked that we are not the same kind of Amish that they were. Uncle Chriss, who had long since left the Amish, said, "Well, I hope not; if you were I would disown you."

1925 swim in the Great Salt Lake of Utah. That's me near the center of the picture and just to the left of the man leaning on the float.

On Monday, July 20, we left Glendive, Montana, arriving in Cody, Wyoming, on July 21 at 7:15 and entered Yellowstone Park by the Cody Road. We traveled through the park by bus and stayed in the cabins overnight. We were thrilled by the animals—elk, bear, buffalo, coyotes—the geysers and hot springs and the wild scenery.

Salt Lake City, Utah, was our goal on Saturday and Sunday, July 25-26. On Saturday we swam in Great Salt Lake. On Sunday we went to the Mormon Church and saw the tabernacle and other sights involved in the history of the Mormon center. I found most of it very strange. But I could only consider it all from my Amish viewpoint.

The swim in the Salt Lake was easier to grasp. Many years later I had a swim in the Dead Sea which I liked better than the Salt Lake. We left Salt Lake City by train and traveled through the Royal Gorge Canyon of Colorado, arriving in Colorado Springs in the evening.

During our stay at Colorado Springs, we spent several

days picnicking with Iowa folks. Together, we went to the Cave of the Winds, Seven Falls, the Petrified Forest, and Pikes Peak. We made an effort to walk up to the Peak, but because of a rainstorm we stopped at the Halfway House and used washtubs for umbrellas. We also visited the Garden of the Gods in the evening. We left Colorado Springs on Friday, July 31 and arrived in Hutchinson, Kansas, on Saturday noon.

We went to the home of John Yoder, one of the fellows who used to stay at our home on weekends when he worked in the foundry in Reading. We attended the Amish church on Sunday and a singing in the evening. John Yoder took me to see a wild animal drive. The drive consisted of a scattering of men around four sections or two square miles. When the signal was given, everyone started walking toward the center, twelve men to a mile-wide area. The animals moved ahead of the drive. As they approached the center point of the drive, they flushed out the coyotes and jack rabbits and shot them. They were looking for a wildcat but didn't find one.

From August 8 through August 12, we visited with Anna Glick's friends and relatives in Indiana. After returning home from our western trip, we were soon in the regular farm routine again—picking tomatoes, harvesting cabbage, and gathering beet seed stalks into the barn for drying.

11.

My Work in the Mid-1920s

In 1924 I farmed the cannery farm on a share basis, using Dad's equipment. Preparations for the farming year included many things. Harnesses needed to be repaired and greased. And the mules were clipped to shed their winter coat. This was a real chore before the day of the electric clipper. Horses and mules were clipped with a hand-powered machine. It was necessary to keep the animal restrained because it usually objected strenuously and tried to kick. The restraint was accomplished either by tightening a twitch on the animal's nose or by tying up a front leg. A horse or mule standing on three legs would lose its balance if it tried to kick.

Clover seed was usually sown in the wheat field in February or early March using a hand-powered broadcaster. This was best done when the ground was slightly frozen and honeycombed on a windless morning.

The stable manure that had been stored in the barnyard over the winter had to be hauled out into the fields. It was all loaded by hand with a manure fork.

It was standard practice for many farmers to attend the farm auctions for farming implements. Auctions were usually held in March. They were an everyday event during the sale season and provided opportunity to visit with other farmers. As social events, they were important. Especially for men.

The young fellows went to farm sales eagerly, even though they had no thought of buying anything except at the huckster's lunch counter. Corner ball was the attraction. It was played in the barnyard after a deep layer of clean straw had been spread over the manure pile. A very fast-moving form of dodge ball, it is played with a homemade tape-covered ball. The ball is soft to minimize injury. But it can sting when thrown hard. And that's the only way it's thrown after it has been passed from corner to corner to be "hot." The game goes on most of the day with new players replacing those who drop out to go eat or watch the horses being sold.

✦ ✦ ✦

On April 5, 1924, I helped David Grabers from Indiana to unload their boxcar-load of furniture and farming implements. Their dog had also arrived in the rail car. Mrs. Graber was a niece of our neighbor Johnny Zook.

Not long after their move from Indiana, the Grabers' dog disappeared. Sometime later they received a letter from a former neighbor in Indiana stating their dog had returned home. How the dog found the way home to Indiana after making the trip to Pennsylvania in a boxcar remains a mystery.

✦ ✦ ✦

That spring I helped with the greenhouse work at home and at Smoketown until the farm work season. The month of April was exceptionally wet and cool. We started our own tomato plants for field planting. This took special care because of frost. The beds needed ventilation during the day. That would mean that we had to carry the cold frame sash off in the morning and cover the beds again in the evening, or take a chance of a frost. If it got cold enough for a frost, we would sometimes get up at two in the morning and carry the sash to cover our tomato plants. It was critical. Our tomato crop was dependent on these plants.

✦ ✦ ✦

We also planted cabbage. Cabbage production in those years was a bit hectic because of market uncertainty. If one shipped a carload of cabbage to New York City on commission, one was responsible for the freight if the cabbage didn't bring enough to pay the freight. I once sent two cars of cabbage to New York City. Too late I discovered the market was glutted those several days. The first carload didn't bring enough to pay the freight. The second car brought enough to pay the freight for both cars, but there was no margin left over. This was an expensive education. I produced the crop but did not realize a penny for the effort. The remainder of the cabbage crop was marketed locally and sold to the Lancaster Vinegar Co. for sauerkraut. It was trucked to Lancaster by Elmer Landis.

12.

Mother's Death and Our Marriage

On October 2, 1925, Mother went to bed in the afternoon, very sick after having had dinner with the family. Mother's health had been failing for several years. But now she went to bed to stay until death. Her bed was on the back porch where there were windows that could be opened for fresh air. Dad had added this room to the east end of the house because of Mother's tuberculosis.

The month of October 1925 was difficult for Mother because of her illness. It had only three fully clear days. There was much rain with no frost until the middle of the month. On the 30th it snowed all day. The next morning the temperature was at 20 degrees with the ground covered with snow.

Mother's condition continued to worsen until she left us for a better home on November 15. During her illness, it was noteworthy to see how many friends, church families, and relatives came to comfort her. Her visitors included her brother, Ben Beiler, with whom she was able to be reconciled, in spite of the fact he had pronounced the *Bann* on her for joining the more liberal Peachy or Beachy Amish church.

The serenity with which Mother awaited and looked forward to her going home was marvelous. I had one afternoon alone with her. It was a precious time. One audible prayer of Mother's I especially cherish was, "*Herr Jesu Christ, an meinem end, befehl ich meine Seele in deiner Hände*" (Lord Jesus Christ, at my end, I give my soul into thy hands). Like the Apostle Paul, she had finished her course (II Tim. 4:7).

The funeral was held on November 16, 1925, at the Weavertown Brethren Church, as Mother had suggested. At her request the German message was by John A. Stoltzfus and the English one by John A. Kennel. Moses Riehl led a private family service at the house.

Moving On

In 1926 young people from the midwestern Amish groups continued coming to Lancaster County. Some came for jobs, but most came to visit. Anna Glick, my future wife, came on February 18. She took a job in Dad's Smoketown greenhouse and found a home with my sister Malinda and family in Smoketown.

On June 11 a group of young folks left for western New York state. This included my sister Mary, Mary Yoder, Sadie Glick, Katie Lapp, Henry Lapp, Anna and me, with Clarence Stoltzfus, my brother Jake, and Aaron Blank as drivers. We went in two Model T Fords.

As we were approaching Watkins Glen, New York, around noon, brother Jake asked Aaron Blank to drive the Model T touring car for a while. Jake had cautioned Aaron to go easy on the foot brake and to alternate with the low gear pedal if need be. As we entered Watkins Glen, at the foot of a very steep hill, Aaron suddenly pushed in the low gear pedal too hard and burned out the band. To have it repaired would have involved a long delay so the Ford continued to Niagara Falls and returned to Lancaster with only high gear and reverse. If we couldn't climb a hill on high gear, we would turn around and back up the hill—all this with a full load of six adults. We made it and recorded a trip gas mileage of 28 miles to the gallon.

Wedding Time

On October 10, 1926, my upcoming marriage to Anna Glick was announced at the close of the communion service at the home of Amos Kauffman. The wedding date was October 24. It took place at the regular church service in the home of Dan Kauffman. Bishop John A. Stoltzfus performed the marriage. We were the first couple he married.

It was a bit unusual in that we were married on a Sunday, not a Tuesday or Thursday. But Anna didn't have a family in Pennsylvania to host a wedding for her. The preparations for the reception were made at our home under the management of Dad Glick with the help of other members of the family and friends. There were about 70 people there for dinner on October 24, 1926 after the wedding.

There was quite a surprise for Anna the day before the wedding when her father and two of her sisters, Martha and Ada Glick, came to our place from Iowa for the wedding. She had not expected them. Anna's father and sisters stayed with us, visiting in the community until November 9 when they returned to Iowa by train.

Preparations for keeping house were next. We needed furniture and other things. I went to the Lancaster Vinegar Co. for payment for my cabbage crop. "Oh," they said, "there is no money available at this time."

I said, "When a person gets married, he should be able to get money on his crop to make down payments for furniture." They found money for my account.

I made a down payment on a Queen Anne dining room suite and a bow-end bedroom suite. We purchased other furniture and housekeeping items by attending auctions of household goods in Lancaster City. We also purchased farm machinery.

We put our feet under Dad's table at mealtime until he and his new wife, Leah Zook, moved to the home at the end

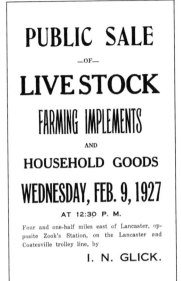

PUBLIC SALE

—OF—

LIVE STOCK

FARMING IMPLEMENTS

AND

HOUSEHOLD GOODS

WEDNESDAY, FEB. 9, 1927

AT 12:30 P. M.

Four and one-half miles east of Lancaster, opposite Zook's Station, on the Lancaster and Coatesville trolley line, by

I. N. GLICK.

HOUSEHOLD GOODS

Prizer range with warming closet, heater, kitchen cabinet, bedsteads, washstands, dresser, extension table, cupboards, chairs, roll top desk, rockers, two bureaus, linoleum, oil cloth, dishes, pails, pans, brooms, power washing machine, wringer, Sharpless cream separator, typewriter, apple and pear butter, by the crock, canned goods, jars, buckets, iron kettle, 4 barrels vinegar, etc., etc.

500 KEIFER PEAR TREES

Sale begins at 12:30 o'clock p. m., on WEDNESDAY, FEBRUARY 9th, when terms and conditions will be made known by the undersigned

I. N. GLICK,

Lancaster, Pa., R. F. D. 6

Beamesderfer & Hacker, Auctioneers, Clerks.

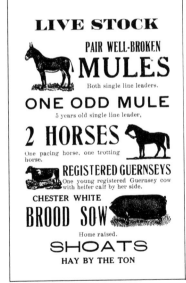

LIVE STOCK

PAIR WELL-BROKEN

MULES

Both single line leaders.

ONE ODD MULE

5 years old single line leader,

2 HORSES

One pacing horse, one trotting horse.

REGISTERED GUERNSEYS
One young registered Guernsey cow with heifer calf by her side.

CHESTER WHITE

BROOD SOW

Home raised.

SHOATS

HAY BY THE TON

FARMING IMPLEMENTS

Jcasey Harris hayloader, side delivery rake, dump rake, Superior disc grain and fertilizer drill, lime and fertilizer drill, Deering binder, Deering 5-foot mower, Osborne 6-foot mower, manure spreader, Black Hawk corn planter, Case Transplanter; Iron Age potato planter, International 2-horse cultivators, 1-horse cultivator, combined roller and harrow, 20-disc harrows, steel roller, tobacco ladders, hayladders.

FARM MACHINERY

Fordson tractor, almost new; 8-horse power gasoline engine and truck, 4-horse power New Way gasoline engine, fodder shredder and carrier, Dellinger chopping mill, circular saw and frame, Ottawa power log and tree saw, concrete mixer, corn sheller, potato sorter, Steward horse clipper, cider mill, wind mill, pulleys, belting, etc., etc.

WAGONS

2-ton Columbian wagon, 2-horse Studebaker wagon, 2-horse Platform spring wagon, market wagon, cart, 2 bob sleds, square back sleigh.

HARNESS

3 sets front gears, yankee harness, driving harness, collars, bridles, lines, flynets, halters, reins, etc.

FIXTURES AND TOOLS

Garden tools, bee hives, platform scales, beam scales, hog feeder, butchering tools, 2 Never break tractor chains, log chains, tripple, double and single trees, hot bed sash, gas tanks, hoes, shovels, carpenter tools, etc.

(upper left) Sale bill front cover; (upper right) Sale bill back cover; (bottom) Sale bill inside.

of the lane of the cannery farm on April 1, 1927.

Prior to the April move, my brother Jake, my wife Anna, and I went into the used furniture business. We bought and renovated used furniture, sanding it down and refinishing it. We planned to sell it at Dad's farm auction, February 9, 1927. Brother Jake would sometimes get so enthused in telling me about his visits with friends while he was traveling, that he would stop sanding the furniture to talk. I would remind him that we must rub and talk. So the expression, "rub and talk," became an inside proverb during the years. We did, however, get all the furniture ready in time for the sale, in spite of time out for conversation.

Before Dad's farm auction, my aunts, Mother's three sisters—aunts Ketty, Lydia, and Susie—came one day to identify and divide to our family the things Mother had gotten from home when she was a bride.

The Farm Auction

I was under obligation to see that Dad's farming equipment which I had been using for several years would be repaired and in condition for his sale. Dad's closing-out farm auction on February 9 was a special event. There was a large crowd and the items sold well in relation to the value of household goods at the time. The sale included the furniture brother Jake and I had refinished. It was a success.

I purchased the pair of mules for $230, a hay wagon for $55, hay loader for $75, and a grain drill for $50. All told, we invested about $600 that day. Later at other farm auctions, I bought a manure spreader for $39, a wheat binder for $79, a wheelbarrow for $3.50, and a tractor plow for $37.50.

The Late 1920s and the Early Years of Our Marriage

Our farming ground during 1927 included Dad's cannery farm where we lived, six acres of corn ground rented from brother Dan, and nearly five acres west on Old Factory Road. We also rented several acres on both sides of what is now Elmwood Road.

Our livestock consisted of a few steers, some hogs, several brood sows, and some shoats, fattened mostly in the corn field. Before the day of the electric fence, I would fence off a small part of the corn field by fastening the woven hog fence to the corn shocks. The corn shocks held up the fence. It was a novel idea, and it worked.

✦ ✦ ✦

During the summer of 1927, the Lincoln Highway was detoured west to Lancaster by way of present Route 896, through Smoketown and the Old Philadelphia Pike to Bridgeport.

Until that time, Eastbrook Road, Route 896, had been little more than a dirt road. Before 1910 it did not even run from Smoketown to the creek. To take care of detour traffic, the road was graded and several inches of crushed rock and blacktop was applied. This took care of the traffic until the spring thaw. Many rural roads were blacktopped this way without stone bottom. We called them Pinchot roads in honor of Governor Pinchot who recognized the need for improved roads (to get the rural folks out of the mud), in spite of limited budgets.

As recently as 1900 there was no bridge across Mill Creek, where Eastbrook Road crosses it, at the site of what is now the Good and Plenty Restaurant. There was a store there, an icehouse, and a very good spring of water. To reach it from Smoketown one drove to the Bird-in-Hand Methodist Church, turned south to a lane leading west along the land of the late Christ Hostetter, and followed the creek to what is now the restaurant.

The 1927 Flood

An equinoctial storm swept over Lancaster County in September 1927, creating general havoc in the entire area. Rain began to fall on a Sunday afternoon, and a cloudburst of 6.5 inches created a situation unprecedented for our area.

The Pequea Creek near Paradise rose by 14 to 15 feet, an all-time record high, at least since the time of Noah. Families

Smoketown under water in September 1927. Glick's Plant Farm is in the background.

were forced to the tops of their houses in Paradise. Many were stranded in cars on flooded roads.

The local situation was complicated by the Lincoln Highway detour, north on present-day Route 896. It was necessary to cross the Mill Creek bridge on the detour. Mill Creek, usually a small stream, rose very suddenly to become wild and turbulent. The bridge was impassable. Water that came up to the running boards of the car—all cars had running boards—suddenly became a wall of water coming into the car windows.

In the meantime, the Old Philadelphia Pike through Smoketown (Route 340) had also flooded. People were stranded because motors flooded out. The situation might best be described as a two-lane traffic jam parked at eleven at night with no motels in sight. The stranded needed lodging. People slept on the floors in nearby houses, wet clothing and all, with hardly any means of drying their clothes.

The Smoketown grocer, Teen Howard, was swamped with customers. He was reported as being practically sold out of everything edible.

A drama was playing itself out just south of my brother David's barn at the corner of routes 340 and 896. Because of the high water, a driver couldn't tell where the road was. He upset his car into a deep ditch. Elsie Glick Kauffman, David's daughter, who was four years old at the time, recalls that lots of people came to her parents' home for shelter the night of the storm. They slept on the floor with others, also stranded. Elsie's mother shared one of Elsie's dresses with a four-year-old girl who had been in the car that upset.

Peril at the Bridge

A Lancaster newspaper reported, "A rescue that had all the color of a sea disaster occurred near Smoketown on Sunday night when the Mill Creek went on a rampage and sent one man up a tree, one of the would-be rescuers up a power line pole, and the other man downstream."

As I remember the episode, Wilmer Weaver, the Strasburg druggist, with his wife and a Miss Groff were heading home after attending church in Lancaster. When Weaver came to the scene of the flood, someone told him other cars had gone through. He tried it, too, and crossed the bridge successfully. But the water over the bridge approach on the far side was deeper than the water over the bridge floor. His motor drowned out and stalled. He was helpless. The women waded out, through water nearly up to their necks. Weaver stayed in the car and tried to get it going. Failing in this, he shucked off some clothes and got ready to swim. The current upset the car and swept him against the fence. He perched on the top rail of the fence for a bit to wait for the water to recede. It was a short wait because the water rose higher and forced him up a tree. The tree was little more than a sapling; the trunk was about as thick as his leg. There he stayed from ten that evening until he was finally rescued at four the next morning.

Two men first attempted a rescue with a boat. Somehow the boat was upset. The one rescuer managed to grab onto a power line pole. His brother was swept downstream with the current. Farther downstream he managed to grab onto some bushes and climb to the bank. The man on the pole had to wait to climb up the pole until the power company could be contacted to turn off the current for that line. He also was stranded on the pole from about ten until four the next morning.

When other efforts at rescue failed, someone contacted the Lancaster City Fire Department. They responded and brought a life line gun and a long length of rope. But the line became entangled and the pin holding the line was lost. So their effort failed, too.

Finally, a man with a life line around his waist, the other end held by others on the bank, was able to wade through and bring both men to safety.

Setting Up Housekeeping

In the early years of our housekeeping, the kitchen range was used to prepare our meals. With only meager income from what we had to sell—eggs at 17 cents a dozen, fat hogs at 11 cents a pound dressed weight, and butter at 20 cents a pound—we thought it best to use wood for fuel. The oil stove was not used regularly because of cost, and bottled gas was not as yet in general use.

Because wood would burn better when dry, my wife Anna would often fill the oven of our kitchen range with wet wood to dry with the heat left over from a cooking fire. At the time, discarded railroad ties were free for the hauling, and I sawed and split some for "range" wood. When it was dry, the wood made the quick, hot fires preferred by cooks in the summer time. Unfortunately, the wood, as obtained, was wet, not dry. Hence the need for drying. One time the wood was drying in the oven too long. It began to smolder and smoke. We were out of the house for the evening. When we came home and opened the door, we were greeted with blue smoke. The kitchen walls and ceiling were blackened with creosote condensate. Fortunately, the door into the living room was closed.

Anna was most anxious to wash the walls and ceiling before Dad could come upon the scene. She was certain he would have been less than enthused with the wood-drying practice, and he was our landlord! Everything worked out all right.

✦ ✦ ✦

For us, farming was a struggle. We soon learned the need for a regular, dependable income. The eggs from our small flock of chickens were often exchanged for groceries at the local store. There was a time in the late '20s when it was difficult to find a market for small lots of eggs, unless you bought groceries for the value of the eggs, but that didn't pay the chicken feed bill.

The shoats and fat hogs didn't provide much of a margin over feed costs, either. I decided to try growing hogs on pasture as it was done in Iowa at that time. I rented about four acres of red clover from my brother Dan to grow some hogs. The creek made a bend along the field. I guessed, wrongly, that the creek would serve as a fence on two sides of the field. The other sides of the field I fenced. Electric fencing was unknown at that time. And I didn't know hogs could swim. Doesn't the Bible give the account of the hogs that drowned in the sea of Galilee? (Mark 5:13)

Imagine my surprise and dismay when in mid-summer I first saw my herd of 30 hogs sunning themselves on the opposite bank of the creek. I located a roll of discarded woven fencing. I was able to stake the fence in the creek several feet from the bank. The hogs couldn't swim through that. The fence, at least, was a success. And growing hogs on clover worked, too. Unfortunately, the hog business didn't meet our need for income at that time.

Butchering Time

If the hogs didn't yield enough income, they did supply our meat. The annual butchering was an important day on every farm. Once a year two or three hogs were slaughtered. A cold winter day was preferred. It was a busy day for both men and women, and neighbors often exchanged help.

Preparation started the day before. Equipment was gotten out, tools were examined to see they were in good order, and knives were sharpened on the hand-cranked grindstone. The scalding trough, meat grinder, sausage stuffer, and bristle scrapers all had to be ready.

A large fire was kindled under the iron kettle in the wash house early in the morning because hot water would be needed as soon as the hog was killed and bled. One needed an early start to complete the work by evening so the hogs were slaughtered by lantern light in the morning. We joked about "sticking the hog with the lantern."

As soon as the hog was bled out, it was lifted into the scalding trough of hot water. The water temperature was critical. If too hot or too cold, the bristles were not readily removed. So the boiling water carried out from the iron kettle was tempered with enough cold water from the pump to bring it to the right temperature. Scraping came next. It was hard work but it took only a few minutes to shave the bristles away. The hog would be placed over a chain in the trough. The chain served to turn the hog over so it could be scraped on both sides. This was part of the men's job.

Next the hog was drawn out of the trough, hoisted on a tripod, washed down, and dressed. After the entrails and internal organs were removed, it was cut in half. The halves were then carried to a butcher bench that was made of a thick slab wood which had peg legs, bringing it to a convenient height.

There the hams, shoulders, and bacons were cut out. The rib meat and any other meat not already removed were put through a meat grinder for sausage. Seasonings such as salt, pepper, and spices were mixed with the ground meat.

Meanwhile, one of the ladies cleaned the entrails. Somehow, the men were not trusted to do the cleaning well enough, and they generally didn't claim competence. The ground meat was pressed into the casings (the cleaned entrails) by a sausage stuffer. The sausages were tied off into links.

Nothing was wasted. The head meat and feet were cooked in the iron kettle with some of the liver to make liver pudding. When the pudding meat was removed from the iron kettle, cornmeal and sometimes wheat middlings or buckwheat flour were stirred into the broth to make scrapple. The kettle was kept boiling away all day until the scrapple was finished. Then the fat meat was heated to render out the lard. When cooked, the fatty portions were put into the lard press to expel the hot liquid lard. The press cake was called the cracklins. Usually, one would eat some of it with salt. Today's low-cholesterol enthusiasts would have been horrified. But most of us who have passed the age of 80 remember the nice flavor. And who knows, the fat meat and butter we consumed may have shortened our lives a lot. But I doubt it.

The hams, shoulders, and bacons were cured. Some people used a dry cure of salt, sugar, and saltpeter. We usually cured our meat in a liquid brine. The brine would be mixed until it was strong enough to float an egg. A fresh egg. Usually the meat stayed in the brine for several weeks.

Smoking sometimes followed. Cured, smoked meat would keep for a long time. The smoking was done in the smokehouse or an attic room by the chimney through which smoke from the wood-fired kitchen range was routed for the smoking period. The smoke had to be cool. Otherwise the lard might melt and drip out of the sausage and bacons.

Some of the meat was preserved in crocks without curing. It was roasted, placed in earthenware crocks, and covered with hot, liquid lard and stored in a cool cellar. Nowadays the method is replaced by canning in glass jars and processing them in boiling water. And even this has largely been replaced by freezing.

✦ ✦ ✦

With all of this effort to use every part of the pig, there was always some waste fat. This fat was carefully saved for soap making at a later time. When enough lard and beef tallow had accumulated, it was put into a big iron kettle and cooked with lye for soap. In my grandmother's day, the lye was made at home by leaching water though wood ashes. By the time Anna was making our soap it was easier to buy "Banner

Lye" at the store.

When the soap had been cooked, it was allowed to cool. The soap would float to the top, and it was then cut into blocks which hardened as they cooled. Underneath the soap layer was a residue of black, offensive liquid which was discarded in the field or garden. Soap making is just a memory now, and not a particularly pleasant one. Grated for use in washing clothes, it was very harsh and not pleasant as a body soap.

Dairy Venture

It soon became evident that we needed a more dependable source of income. In 1927 we had several cows and Anna made butter, for which we found ready sale locally. In the spring of 1928, Anna suggested we start to sell milk from the few cows we had. Our first milk check for the month was $71, the second month $64, and the third month $53. We had our cows tested for tuberculosis and found several reactors. Of course this meant we had to replace them with others.

In August of 1928, Dad and his wife, Leah, made a trip to Missouri, seeking medical treatment. She had cancer. While on their trip, I contacted Dad to buy some cows for us. He was able to buy a carload of grade Holsteins in Minnesota—20 head at $115 a piece. They were the usual run of grade cows and the price was reasonable. We lost several head to shipping fever and for one reason or another, sold most of them again.

Our best success in finding good dairy cows was at close-out farm sales in Belleville in Pennsylvania's Big Valley. There seemed to be less health risk with these cows than with the shipped cows.

In 1929, we installed a milking machine and went into the business of milking cows and raising dairy heifers, a venture that kept us occupied for more than 30 years. We soon decided we should have a purebred Holstein herd. Years later when one formed locally, we joined the Dairy Herd Improvement Association, giving us regular contact with the

Our son Ivan in 1929. Notice the toy rabbit on the running board of the Chandler owned by Anna's brother, Daniel, who spent some time with us that year. The big touring car got about eight miles per gallon. Gas was about six gallons for a dollar.

breeders of good herds in the County.

In our first test year we had a 400-pound butter fat average for the herd. It was thought very good. Exceptional. Now good herds routinely produce two times as much or more.

For the first while we milked our cows by hand and Anna's sister Katie helped us. Ivan was just a little toddler and Katie would take him along to the stable during milking time. One time, as he toddled about he lost his balance and fell into the cow gutter. His clothes were a mess. He was a mess all over. The gutter was nearly full of liquid manure. He needed a bath and a complete change from head to foot. I carried a screaming child to the house, holding him out at arm's length. He was very, very soiled. His mother stood him under a spigot, flushed him off, and bathed him until she could recognize her son again.

A local trucker hauled our milk to the receiving station for the first several years. After my brother David started a dairy, he and I hauled our milk together, alternating days.

I had a Model T Ford touring car converted into a pickup, which I used every other morning rain or shine. Model T Fords could be bought at that time for $35 and sometimes for as little as $10 for a car that would run fine. The milk receiving station was at the railroad station in Ronks. Here one would meet other farmers while waiting to unload. There was time to visit, especially if there was a truck load of milk cans to unload ahead of you. All milk was delivered in 100-pound cans at that time. Later there was a switch to 85-pound, 10-gallon cans. There were no farm bulk tanks until nearly 40 years later. Unfortunately, milk was in surplus at this time and our margins were meager in the early years.

Once when I went to deliver the milk, Anna went along to the grocery store. Having bought her groceries, she was waiting on the porch in front of the store for my return. When I came by, I forgot her and drove on home. When I came home, her sister Katie asked, "Where's Anna?" I was embarrassed.

Automobiles Become More Commonplace

In September of 1928, our church—the Peachy Church (Weavertown Amish Mennonite Church today)—took counsel on whether or not members should be permitted to own cars. Some of us had already purchased one or more. The church service was held at my sister Malinda's home (the Aaron Riehls) in Smoketown. After the service, a congregational vote was taken. Our group decided to accept cars with the requirement that they be black. Like other Amish decision-making, it was a group decision. The vote was nearly 100% in favor of accepting the cars. What had seemed like an impractical rich man's toy a decade earlier had become a practical, acceptable tool. Or, so it seemed.

Two years later the decision to begin holding worship services in the Weavertown meetinghouse was made in the same way.

Our Brand-New Model A and the 1929 Trip to Iowa

During the summer of 1929, Anna, our small son Ivan, and I took a car trip to Iowa. We had a Model T Ford touring car and Anna felt certain it would get us to Iowa. But I was skeptical. Several weeks earlier, Anna's sister Katie had been driving the Model T with little Ivan on the front seat beside her. As Katie turned into our lane, Ivan grabbed hold of the steering wheel to stand up. They ended up in the deep ditch beside the lane. The front end of the Model T was bent. It was a good excuse to buy a new car.

So, in spite of Anna's protest, I bought a brand-new 1929 Model A Ford Tudoor from Kennel Brothers, using our Glick discount. Later, Anna was glad that I had bought a new car. This was the only new car we ever owned. We left sister Katie with the responsibility of caring for the few cows and headed for Iowa.

Driving a car all the way to Iowa at that time was a real event for us. As I remember, we drove to Belleville, Pennsylvania, the first afternoon. After an overnight stay with friends, we drove all the way to Apple Creek, Ohio. There we again visited with friends and left early the next day. We drove to western Illinois and found lodging in a tourist home in Mt. Morris. Motels were not yet part of the scene. A few tourist cabins were available, but only along main routes. The third day we drove the rest of the way to Kalona. Cross-country driving meant going through all the cities and towns and detours along the way. There were no bypasses.

We spent several weeks in Iowa. Anna visited her relatives while I helped with the oat harvest. At that time, grain was harvested with a binder and threshed with steam-powered threshing machines. I well remember helping brother-in-law Chriss shock oats. We made round shocks and spread out a sheaf on top of the shock to turn off the rain. This sheaf was always placed facing the northwest.

During our stay in Iowa I also took several of Anna's aunts to Buchanan County, Iowa, to visit their friends there.

When our visit to Iowa was over, Anna's sister Lydia and

MOTHER'S DEATH AND OUR MARRIAGE

Dennis Miller returned to Lancaster with us. We drove to eastern Indiana (Allen County) to stay with friends for the night. There we met the Pete Stauffers and John Smuckers from Pennsylvania who were also visiting in the community. The next day we made the return trip home, with a stopover in Belleville to buy several cows.

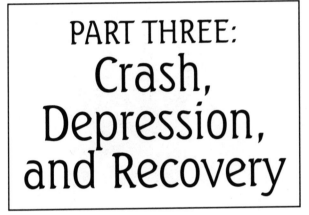

PART THREE:
Crash,
Depression,
and Recovery

13.

The 1929 Stock Market Crash

The Wall Street stock market crash of 1929 led to the Depression of the 1930s. Those were lean years, not only for farmers, but for people in the cities as well. Thousands lost their jobs and buying power. Some were hungry because they had no money to buy food. In the country, surpluses of unsalable farm products demoralized the markets. Many local farmers lost their milk market and sold their cows. In desperation, unemployed workers staged hunger marches and demonstrations in many of the cities.

American farmers had an advantage over their city cousins because they could grow their own food. If there were few luxuries, there was no hunger on the land. But there was pain. There were many bankruptcies. Unless you were debt-free, you had a problem because earning enough to live was a full-time task. Earning enough to pay interest on any debt was a real problem. Like many other farmers, Anna and I hung on as best we could. We learned the meaning of grinding poverty. It is an experience one never quite outlives.

In addition to the economic misery, the 1930s saw dust storms in the Great Plains, after homesteading farmers broke up the prairie grasslands to plant wheat. In the Texas Panhandle the acreage of wheat had increased from 62,000 acres in 1909 to more than five million acres by 1930. The invention of tractors made this possible. World War I wheat prices made it profitable. There was ample rainfall at that time. By 1931, the wheat yield was sometimes up to 50 bushels per acre because the fertility of the new land had not yet been exhausted.

There were not enough barns, grain elevators, and railroad cars to hold all the wheat. There weren't enough people to buy it. The price collapsed. No longer a dollar a bushel, it fell to a mere 25 cents per bushel, not enough to cover costs. The surplus of wheat had a profound effect on our local economy. The price of soft red Pennsylvania winter wheat dropped from $1.32 a bushel in 1928 to 49 cents a bushel by 1932. Local farmers who depended on wheat as their cash crop were in real difficulty. Then a dry weather cycle followed the moist cycle, and life on the Plains was a disaster.

14.

A Farm
of
Our Own

1931 was our last year on the cannery farm. Brother David and I went together to rent some additional ground that year—the Stauffer farm at Witmer. This included the farmhouse which we sublet to William Nagle. As I recall, he paid little, if any, rent because he was out of work. Most of the field work was done by Amos Lapp and Perry Bontrager, our hired hands. We invested in some beef cattle to feed the corn crop. It was a rather dry summer, and our final profit for the year was the use of the farm, $0.00. Brother Daniel took over my part of the Stauffer farm the following year.

◆ ◆ ◆

On April 30, 1931, we made early morning bonfires to keep the frost off our tomato plants. Later, after the tomatoes were planted in the field, we had to put a little bran mixed with Paris Green at each stalk because of the cutworms. It was an arsenic chemical, a deadly poison that remains in the soil a long time. Some of it could still be there!

In history, arsenic was used to murder people. It was real hard on cutworms. Other, safer insecticides are available now that can be applied with a sprayer. But in 1931 the state-of-the-art control involved manual, plant by plant, application. One put on a lot of miles trudging down the rows.

We planted our corn at home on the cannery farm on May 20. We had kept the Fordson tractor going all night to prepare the land for planting. With no lights on the tractor, Edwin Miller tied a lantern to the front for enough light to steer by.

✦ ✦ ✦

During these years, Anna and I had a driving desire to have a farm of our own. At one time, we signed papers with Dad to buy the cannery farm. But he changed his mind and canceled the contract. We also had seriously considered moving to Iowa as Anna's dad had offered us his farm. But we dismissed those plans, too. The Depression was discouraging.

✦ ✦ ✦

"Go along to the sale tomorrow?" Pete Stauffer said to me one February day in 1932. So the following day we headed for a farm implement sale in West Lampeter Township just across the Strasburg Pike.

Located along a nameless dirt road with no telephone poles and grass growing in the center between the wheel tracks, the farm was along what is now Rockvale Road. We drove in through the field and parked. Here was a nice level farm with a good log house and an old barn in poor condition. A straw stack stood in front of the barn and a stone wall went around the barnyard. An old dilapidated corn barn was built against the west gable end of the barn. A wagon shed was built against the northwest side of the barn. There was no silo. The stable had old-style stalls with wooden-spoke hayracks above the wooden feed troughs. The farm had no electricity.

A FARM OF OUR OWN

On the day of the sale, I heard the farm itself was also for sale. Nearly 70 acres for $8,000. I was interested immediately because I thought this was a farm at a price that we could eventually pay for. But alas! I didn't know how poor the soil was. Nor did I know the extended Depression years we would be facing.

I went home that day all enthused about buying the farm. I could hardly wait until I could tell my Anna about the farm and its opportunity for us. We inquired further, and the following day went to look at the farm. Anna was interested. But some arrangements had to be made before we could buy. We needed to see if Dad would allow us to leave his farm so close to spring time. We needed to make arrangements with brother David concerning the Stauffer farm which we were renting on shares. And we needed mortgage money for the farm. We were able to work out all these things and buy the farm within a week of the auction, the day I first saw the farm!

I was as happy as a little boy with a new toy. We began to make plans for improvements as soon as we made the down payment, even though we could not make settlement until October.

The necessary renovation at the barn was soon planned and managed by Dad. It seemed there was hardly anything he enjoyed as much. I was able to begin work on the stable almost immediately. This was a priority so we could move our cows and other livestock in and be able to sell milk from the farm. To get electricity to run our milking machine, water pump, and lights, we had to hook up our own electric line down to the lower end of the farm. We also had to give the electric company a guarantee of ten dollars a month for electric service.

It was Dad's idea to get short poles and build a low line along the fencerow to our house. It happened that a March ice storm broke down many poles along the Old Philadelphia Pike. We were able to get some of those poles, which we cut short, fitting our needs.

We moved the springhouse closer to the barn where it

served as a milkhouse. There was hardly any money available, even to buy building materials, so we had to work things out with the materials on hand. The silo was a second-hand structure we moved in and erected. A storm blew in the one side when it was first erected.

Since there was no plumbing in the house, we used the old woodshed for a bathroom. It had a fireplace at one end with a hanging iron kettle that was used to heat water for our bath. The shed was warmed by the fire that heated the water. The outside toilet, common at that time, was used until we were able to afford a bathroom many years later. The spring was an appreciated item because it provided a good supply of water. There was a hand-dug well at the end of the arch cellar below the basement level of the house.

15.

The Depression
and
How We Coped

The summer of 1932 was very dry. We didn't get any hay crop. The field that we depended on for hay was only a short white clover which didn't grow tall enough to produce any hay. We used part of the wheat crop for pasture in addition to the hay (clover) field. The wheat crop was average but the corn hardly yielded enough to fill the silo.

We bought several loads of alfalfa hay from John Smucker that I found I couldn't pay for. We finally gave him our leghorn pullets which Anna had raised for layers, thus paying for the hay. We bought several truck loads of corn fodder in bundles which we fed to the cows instead of hay. We were also able to get pea vine silage from the pea huller. This was the stalk residue of the pea vines which were put on a pile as the peas were hulled. We left some corn on shocks to grind with the hammer mill as cattle feed. This finely ground whole-plant corn roughage was very good feed.

In addition to our cows we had a few hogs. I remember selling weaned shoats to Jay Mellinger for 50 cents each.

(top) We moved a sugar maple (tied up and heavily trimmed in the foreground) from the cannery farm to our new home in 1932. Note Fordson tractor beside the house.

(bottom) 1928 Model A with a Karikeen trunk. I used this car to haul our milk cans (note cans in the trunk) to the Ronks receiving station for Suplee Wills Jones milk company. I am holding Ada Marie with Ivan standing beside me.

THE DEPRESSION AND HOW WE COPED

✦ ✦ ✦

In our first years on the farm, we moved our kitchen stove into the middle room during the winter months. The only heat we had in the house was provided by this coal stove and its stovepipe that passed through the upstairs bedroom.

There was no money for the luxury of central heat. We had to depend almost entirely on the tiny milk check! And sometimes the pay was as low as 70 cents for 10 gallons. Later we heated the middle room with an oil heater until we installed hot water heat with radiators after World War II.

In our early years on the farm, we continued to deliver our milk to the receiving station at Ronks with our Model T Ford. Later we used our Model A Ford Tudor with a Karikeen trunk that could be closed for Sunday driving.

Producing enough feed for our dairy cattle took a real effort. We usually tried to plant corn to grow a crop for the silo after barley harvest. A bit later we also grew soybeans and sorghum. Since the modern machines to harvest sorghum were not yet in existence, we cut the forage with the mower and loaded it with the pushbar-type hay loader and forked the stuff into the ensilage cutter to blow into the silo. This made a large tonnage of good feed in any year with enough rainfall, but I stopped growing it because loading it in the field and handling it was very hard work.

✦ ✦ ✦

It was the worst economic depression in the history of the United States. Millions of people were continuing to lose jobs. The deep discontent it brought had swept Franklin D. Roosevelt into office as President with his promise of a New Deal for everyone in 1932.

The Agricultural Adjustment Act (AAA) was passed on May 12, 1933. Its goal was to restore prices so farmers would have the same purchasing power they had between 1909-1914. Farmers were asked to keep a portion of their cropland out of production or to plow down a specific portion of crop. The government would pay the farmer for the land not in produc-

(top) The barn on our Rockvale Road farm. This view is from the south after we closed the forebay and removed the dung-yard wall.

(bottom) Ada Marie at about three years of age.

THE DEPRESSION AND HOW WE COPED

Cousins: Left to right, Evan Riehl, our Ada Marie, Lena, Edna, and Aquilla Riehl, and in the cart, Melvin, John Lewis, Elmer, and Dannie. Ivan is holding the pony. The pony was Anna's idea for her son. The idea didn't really "take" because the pony had a nasty disposition. I built the cart using a piece of pipe for the axle, old cultivator wheels, and some old boards for the box. The harness was a cut-down horse harness.

tion. The government also set a guaranteed price per bushel for crops grown by farmers who cooperated. It helped, but it didn't restore prosperity. That only came with World War II.

The average open-market price for farm produce during 1929-1933 was 35 cents a bushel for corn, 50 cents a bushel for wheat, and 75 cents per 100 lbs. of milk delivered at the receiving station. Eggs were 17 cents a dozen.

Many people came to farms looking for work. However, our income often barely enabled us to break even at the end of the year. One farmer, our friend John Smucker of Bird-in-Hand, said that all he had to show for the year's work was his new false teeth. He was fortunate because many farmers found themselves deeper in debt at year end.

✦ ✦ ✦

After the first several dry years, rainfall in the 1930s became more normal. Then we found out that we had wet

Big brother Ivan shows off for admiring sister Ada Marie.

spots in some fields; places where there were springs. That made it necessary to put drain tile underground to drain out the excess water. Since there were no funds to rent a machine for laying tile, I asked our county agent, Floyd Bucher, to survey the wet spots and make a plan to place the tile.

I plowed the first depth, then took a shovel and tile spade and made the ditches deep enough to drain the underground springs. I bought 3,000 four-inch drain tiles from Lloyd Winey, who had used them to bleach celery. I guess I laid them all myself. Today, after 50 years, the water continues to flow through those tiles and keeps the fields drained.

THE DEPRESSION AND HOW WE COPED

✦ ✦ ✦

Our farm work in the years before World War II was accomplished with horses and a Fordson tractor. In the mid 1930s a 10-20 McCormick Deering tractor replaced the Fordson. The McCormick was easier to start and seemed to have more pulling power. But one day a connecting rod came out through the side of the block as I was disking.

It was critical. Planting time was upon us. We looked at several tractors, including an Allis Chalmers WC, a Farmall F-20, and a David Bradley. We finally bought a John Deere A tractor for its belt power and because it was uncomplicated. It was a one-year-old demonstrator and the price was reasonable. Anna was pleased that it had a platform if the driver would choose to stand. She realized our 12-year-old Ivan would now be driving tractor. The earlier steel wheel tractors were harder to steer, too much for a 12-year-old.

16.

Our Depression-Era "Vacations"

In July 1931, Anna, little Ivan, and I visited church friends in the Grantsville, Maryland, community. During this time, Ivan caught the measles. This extended our stay a little longer than planned. We had the privilege of staying at the home of Noah Brenneman near the Conservative Children's Home, which Noah had established as a home for orphans.

The orphanage had its beginning in 1913 in the Brenneman home. When it outgrew that facility, it moved to a new building on a nearby hill. It cared for 560 children during the 24 years of its existence.

Funding was always a problem. The Brennemans and other Amish Mennonites in the area had very little more than their sincere desire to help the unfortunate children who had lost parents and were left with no one to love and care for them. Feeding and clothing the children was a struggle for these folks as many of them had very little themselves.

While we were there, we decided to have Margaret Fallon, one of the teenage girls, come share our home and be Anna's helper. She lived with us for an extended period. I think she was often sad even though we tried to make her feel accepted. But we decided against adoption and returned her to the orphanage. Later she found a home in Big Valley without adoption papers.

Increasingly, funding became a serious problem and the New Deal programs provided some alternatives for the less fortunate. The orphanage was closed in 1938. Today the facility is a home for senior citizens. Noah Brenneman served as leader throughout the years it functioned as an orphange.

✦ ✦ ✦

In August of 1931, Anna's father, John A. Glick, visited us. When he left us to go back to Iowa, he planned a stopover in the Big Valley, near Belleville where "Indian John," our Glick ancestor, had lived generations earlier.

While visiting in the Valley, he suffered a breakdown and became mixed up in his mind. We brought him back to our home. It was soon apparent that he needed to be taken home to Iowa where longer-term care would be available. So on August 15, Jacob Troyer along with my father and me made a hurried trip to Iowa in Dad's 1930 Ford with my father-in-law under partial restraint.

Jacob Troyer had a way of keeping him under control when he became unruly during the driving. The first day we drove to the home of Dan Glick near Goshen, Indiana. Dan was my father-in-law's brother. We stayed there overnight. The next day we drove all the way through to Kalona, by way of Iowa City.

The three of us stayed in Iowa over the weekend visiting my in-laws. Then we headed home. The first day we made it to Berlin, Ohio, about bedtime, planning to stay with Jacob Troyer's brother. It was not until after midnight that we were able to locate his home. Our only clue was that he got his mail on the Dundee rural postal route. Finding his home in the Holmes County, Ohio, hills after bedtime was a never-to-be-forgotten experience. At about 2 a.m. we finally found him.

We made the drive home the next day. Dad did his share of the driving in spite of his handicap. My brother Jake had rigged the car so he could handle both clutch and brake of the standard gearshift drive with just one leg. His wooden leg was useful for walking but of no use in the car.

The same trip would occupy fewer than half the hours now, thanks to highway improvement. The new highway system would have pleased my father. His good leg had a heavy foot.

After treatment and a few years care in the Iowa State Hospital at Mt. Pleasant, Anna's father was able to take his place in the home again.

❖ ❖ ❖

In 1936, Anna and I and our family had the privilege of taking a trip to Anna's former Iowa home, through the courtesy of Amos Kauffman and his wife, Sue, who drove their Dodge car. The drive to Iowa was a three-day journey. We stayed with Amish friends near Hartville, Ohio, and Nappanee, Indiana, on the way. On the way home we stopped over with friends in Indiana and Mercer County, Pennsylvania.

Because we stayed with friends, the trip cost very little. Otherwise it would not have been possible for us. This manner of travel saved the cost of meals and accommodation. More importantly, it served to extend the horizons of friendship and community. The hosts would be our guests at another time. In some cases, they had been welcomed in our home at an earlier time.

❖ ❖ ❖

A trip to Knoxville, Tennessee, to see the place "Tennessee" John Stoltzfus, my great-grandfather, had settled came a year later in 1937. While there, we stayed with the William Jennings family. Mrs. Jennings was able to show us where our ancestor had lived and where he and his wife were buried near Concord.

We stopped to see the newly built Tennessee Valley Authority Norris Dam, toured northern Kentucky, and drove to Goshen, Indiana, where we visited the Isaiah Royer family. Mrs. Royer was a cousin of my mother, also a descendant of "Tennessee John." Our daughter, Ada Marie, had come on the scene on June 4, 1933, and with her older brother, Ivan, added zest to this trip.

✦ ✦ ✦

In January 1942, shortly after Pearl Harbor, Congress gave the Office of Price Administration (OPA) the power to ration scarce commodities and to set ceiling prices on many items. If the war was giving the economy a boost, there was no intention of letting inflation run rampant.

The OPA, issuing books of varied colored ration stamps to everyone, rationed many things. Autos, rubber, steel, fuel, and some food. Beef, butter, coffee, and sugar were rationed. Shoes and tires were controlled.

Scrimping and conniving quickly became very normal. We had tires retreaded because they couldn't be replaced. Housewives dealt with bunches of coupons of changing values and were careful to get them cashed in before expiration dates.

Obtaining gasoline was a major headache. In the beginning some people managed to get "X" cards for unlimited gas purchase. It was resented when congressmen and others with "pull" had "X" car stickers for unlimited gas purchase. By contrast, most drivers had to use either "A," "B," or "C" coupons, which restricted them to different amounts of gas purchases. The "A" cardholder was eligible for only a few gallons per month.

A mobster ring sold fake "C" coupons until it was nabbed. There seemed to be plenty of black market gas for some people. The OPA had help from the Justice Department and the Secret Service, but no sympathy from the public who was being denied gas for its cars.

But despite its problems, the OPA somehow worked. At least we survived it. Most folks managed. Scarce supplies were stretched. It was unfortunate if a tractor or manure spreader tire blew out. To get permission to buy a replace-

Jay Elvin, Ada Marie, and a somewhat dubious little Catherine (Katchi).

ment you had to go to the ration board in town to apply for a permit. Permits were not surrendered willingly.

One man with experience claimed that the bureaucrats filled out the papers faster when he went to the OPA office for a manure spreader tire permit without bathing or changing clothes.

It was said President Harry Truman tried to keep the OPA in force after the war's end, but Congress so weakened it that the agency was eliminated. After the war, most things quickly became abundant, and cars roared down the roads again. But only old cars because it took a while for manufacturers to convert back to civilian production from war work.

OUR DEPRESSION-ERA "VACATIONS"

✦ ✦ ✦

During the war years, any unnecessary driving, even a visit to one's friends on Sunday, was frowned upon. It was suggested that families should attend the church nearest to their home regardless of denomination to avoid "waste in religion."

In some ways, the situation was a repeat of the World War I period I remembered as a boy. One major difference, however, involved the provisions made for pacifists, especially conscientious objectors, who refused military service. They were relegated to special Civilian Public Service (CPS) work camps as a substitute for military service. The young men drafted into this service were not paid and had to be supported by their home church congregations. Food at these camps was rationed, perhaps unnecessarily, and was sometimes donated by various churches.

It so happened that Anna and I found out about a shipment of food from Lancaster County which was to be sent to a CPS camp at Dennison, Iowa, west of Anna's home community. Someone needed to drive the truck for the delivery. If we could make the delivery, Anna would be able to visit her family in Iowa.

That's how we were able to get gas ration stamps for fuel to take a pickup load of canned fruit to the CPS camp in western Iowa. My brother Jacob let us use the Glick's Plant Farm pickup to make the trip. Our son Ivan stayed home with our farm and to take care of Jay Elvin, who was born on July 29, 1938. Elvin was an autistic epileptic.

Daughters Kathy, who was born on February 6, 1941, and Ada Marie, along with their mother, visited our people in Kalona. Kalona minister Albert Miller and I took the load of food to the CPS camp at Fort Dennison.

After a weekend visit in Kalona, we loaded the pickup with some bags of shelled corn and some household goods for Mrs. Sam Yoder of Stuarts Draft, Virginia, and started home. Corn was in scarce supply in Lancaster County at that time. Our first stop was at Sterling, Illinois, with the parents of

Little Jay Elvin checks out his reflection in our 1936 Ford.

Paul Wade, who had stayed with us as a CPS dairy tester. After an overnight visit there, we started early for Hartville, Ohio. There we stayed at the home of minister Roman Miller overnight. The next night we made the drive home. We had a flat tire on the Pennsylvania turnpike west of Harrisburg. Brother Jake had to drive up from Smoketown to help us. It would have been better not to have loaded our pickup quite as heavily for our return trip.

17.

Life
in the
1940s

Our Farming Experiences During the 1940s

One winter in the late 1940s our three horses died. It was an odd thing. The vet told us the problem was forage poisoning. I'm not sure if he really knew. It was surmised that the horses had inadvertently gotten some fermented silage, perhaps with the sweepings of the feedway that were thrown into the horse stalls for bedding.

With the horses gone, we learned how to do all our farm work with a tractor. By now we had hybrid corn that had better stalk and root strength so we could cut all our field corn with the corn binder. The bundles stood up on large shocks to dry.

Later, they were brought to the barn with the buckrake and put through the husker-shredder which we owned in partnership with a neighbor, William Myers. The husker-shredder husked the ears of corn out and shredded the corn stalks for bedding. It took much less labor than hand husking.

The buckrake was a homemade contraption mounted on the back of an old Model A truck chassis that had seen service at the cannery farm. We built it during World War II. It worked a bit like a front-end loader on a tractor but was raised and lowered by a cable winch instead of hydraulics. It was ten feet wide with iron-tipped wooden prongs twelve feet long.

Our buckrake was one of several built in Lancaster County. In the west they mounted them on old Buicks and used them to bring grass hay to stacking areas. I had an idea we could use them for that here. But the thing didn't really work out for alfalfa. As a corn shock mover, it replaced several wagons, tractors, and a crew of field workers. We kept it until we switched to the corn picker from the husker-shredder.

Pickers didn't gain acceptance here until the baler and stalk shredders made it feasible to gather corn stalks for bedding. Further west where farmers didn't want to save their corn fodder, the picker had already replaced the husker-shredder.

✦ ✦ ✦

The value of good hay was much appreciated here. But making good hay was a problem. Frequent rains during curing time often ruined the crop. Haybines (stem crushers) were unknown. Beginning in 1943, we experimented with the barn hay finisher. It used a fan to blow air up through the hay. A mow full of partly dried hay would finish drying in a matter of days, depending on the temperature and humidity. It was a way to beat the weather. Pioneered by the Tennessee Valley Authority before the war, the system was quite practical.

After we saw the benefits on our farm, we became dealers for the systems. We sold quite a few of these fan outfits until other methods were developed to dry the hay faster in the field and hay crop silages were better understood. As herds expanded, more dairymen used the silo to store more of their hay crop because the weather-risk interval was much

The hay drying fan was an innovation in 1944. That's me on the right with the fan in our barn. After using one on our farm, Anna and I decided to become dealers. We sold quite a few of these machines, many of which are still being used.

shorter than for cured hay. Even so, many of the systems purchased through us are still in use 40 years later. Often it is one of the grandsons of the original purchaser who is using it now.

✦ ✦ ✦

When hybrid corn came on the scene, a real demand for corn binders in Lancaster County developed suddenly.

Anna with our daughter, Catherine, in front of the old Othello range where she cooked many a wonderful dish.

Thanks to the wartime shortage of steel, new binders were not available. But in Iowa, corn pickers had replaced the binders. There the binders and stationary husker-shredders were obsolete and idle. Ivan talked with his uncles in Iowa and arranged the shipment of three train carloads of used corn binders and a few husker-shredders. They arrived in Bird-in-Hand in 1945 and were easily sold. The proceeds just covered the cost of blacktopping our farm lane.

In 1947-48 there was something else stirring on our

Anna found ways to keep the children busy because talent shouldn't go to waste. Here she is in our kitchen with Ada Marie and Catherine.

farm. We never knew what was ahead, but we found life exciting and full of challenges. The Dellinger Manufacturing Co. of Lancaster was fussing with a forage harvester to chop crops in the field. It had its own engine, didn't need a tractor power-take-off, and worked with smaller tractors. The machine successfully replaced the corn binder and saved a lot of hand labor. They did a lot of the experimenting on our

We tested the 1949 New Holland Model 600 harvester on our farm. This photo appeared in their first sales brochure.

farm with son Ivan's help.

Dellingers finally sold out to the New Holland Machine Company, using the performance of the forage harvester as an excuse for the transaction. There would have been no reason for New Holland to purchase their line of already-obsolete stationary silage choppers. However, the forage harvester was the wave of the future.

◆ ◆ ◆

One day in 1949 I was out disking in the field north of the road and neighbor Steve Boshnagle came out to talk to me. He told me that the neighboring Dan Brook farm, then owned by Matt Vital, had been sold to macaroni millionaire Mueller. However, the deal had fallen through and the farm was now for sale again. Boshnagle thought maybe I would buy it. I guess I said, "Of course not." But as I got to thinking about it, I began to consider this move. I am sure I talked to the Lord about it, but I don't understand even to this day how it all came to pass. When I came into the house, I talked to

The Dan Brook farm, which we purchased in 1949 and resold in 1959.

Anna about it and she seemed agreed to consider the project. So I made them an offer.

The sale included the year's crops, the implements, the barn with the three silos, a poultry house for laying hens, a mansion house, and a tenant house with a large shed for $80,000. It was an unheard-of sum.

We sold the mansion farmhouse to William Musser and the tenant house across the road to the Hubers. That reduced the debt by more than half. We owned the farm for ten years until we sold it to John Glick for his son, Elam. In the meantime we built three houses along the west end of the farm frontage for sale.

We also bought the John Neff farm along the Lampeter Road. Here we sold the frontage along the Windy Hill Road to several individuals, and the farmhouse and barn to Ira Nafziger. It was during this time that Ivan made the acquaintance of Joe Hull, who had an important position in the New Holland Machine Company. Subsequently, he hired Ivan for a job there that would last for the next 24 years.

Our Experiences with Sunnyside Mennonite Mission Church

Sometime in the 1940s, we began to attend midweek prayer meetings with the Sunnyside Mennonite Mission Church near Lancaster. These meetings were often held in the homes of unchurched folks who lived on the hill, a sort of shantytown.

Those who assumed responsibility for these meetings were David High, Walter Herr, Witmer Barge, pastor Jacob Harnish, and several other dedicated workers. Folks were being saved during their revival meetings. There were usually also classes for the children from the hill.

I remember a Mrs. Gainor. On the evening she responded to the altar call, she reached over to one of the other pews and called her husband to "Come along, Harry, you need salvation, too." Her deep dedication and sincerity continues in my memory.

✦ ✦ ✦

There were others who likewise had real testimonies; people like Perry Stoughton who once told us his life story. He had gone west and worked on a ranch around the turn of the century. One of the group of cowpunchers with whom he worked decided to join the rustlers and make some easy money by rustling cattle, even from the ranch where they worked.

Perry told us how they caught up with the cowboy and hanged him. "I can still see his blue eyes as he hung there." In those days, life on the range was wild. But Perry also said the best of life for him was when he found salvation and peace with the Lord at Sunnyside. Attending Sunnyside midweek meetings was an opportunity for group Bible study that we did not have at that time in our home congregation— the Peachy church which had by then been meeting in a church house near Weavertown for many years.

Our Experiences with Homeless People in the 1940s

Many homeless people came to our farm through the years. They were an interesting assortment. Each was an individual in his own right. And in one way or another, they enriched our lives. For reasons that are less than clear, these wanderers were all men. Some were alcoholic, some mentally affected in one way or another, and some were both. Anna took them all in and fed them. They were accepted more or less on their own terms. But Anna had her sense of propriety, too.

To her, it seemed that one should give something in exchange for food. So she would put them to work splitting firewood while she prepared the meal, even if she didn't particularly need the wood. It seemed only proper so the "guest" would not think of himself as a beggar. His self-respect should be preserved.

Sometimes we offered them work for wages if it seemed appropriate. I remember one harmless fellow named Davy. If Davy had a last name, he never divulged it. He consumed phenomenal volumes of food. I put him to work cleaning the cow stable. After a few hours, he asked for his wages and left. He had calculated that he would have earned enough for a few beers or some whiskey, and since that was the objective, there was no incentive to work longer.

Another wanderer was from the Kentucky hills. He knocked at the door saying he was looking for a certain Stoltzfus family where he might find work. As it turned out, he decided to help us. No matter what task, he continually held a spirited conversation with himself. Sometimes he would sing hymns in full voice and then break out in shouted profanity. But his work was satisfactory. After a while, he decided to head back to Kentucky. He had one special concern. He worried how he could get through Harrisburg without being picked up by the police and taken to the state mental hospital. Apparently, he had some experience.

One of the more memorable was Louis Gohr. He was an Illinois or Ohio native who ran away from home as a youth and had never gone back. He worked for us for several months during World War II. When he was ready to leave, he offered to let me examine his suitcase so I could see that he hadn't stolen anything. I refused the favor.

Later we discovered he usually worked a trick when he

was ready to move on. Upon collecting his wages, he would negotiate an advance for some excuse or another and would go to town and just disappear.

Some of the men were local. There was a man from Lancaster named Landis. Anna's cooking agreed with him much better than our chores. A man by the name of Bowman who had somehow lost touch with reality was brought to us. He was an expert lettering artist. His stay extended over a period of months. Living with us on the farm as part of the family, he regained his health. Participating in his healing was a real blessing for us, too. The blessings of service have to be experienced to be understood. Our Lord was right when he said, "It is more blessed to give than to receive."

But the most memorable of all the homeless was Warren Duburrow. One day in the late 1940s bishop Stoner Kready of the Vine Street Mennonite Mission brought him to us and asked if we would give him a temporary home until he recovered from a gunshot wound in the head. Just out of the hospital, with no home and not able to work and little to lose, he had wandered into the Mission. When the altar call was given, he stood for Jesus. Of course, the preacher couldn't just turn him back out on the street so he brought him to us.

He moved in. On Wednesday evening I offered transportation to the Mission for the midweek prayer meeting. He responded that he'd really like to go but that he was too tired. To the best of my recollection, he was never sufficiently rested to go to church again. But he quickly assumed the role of grandfather to all of us.

Warren was exceptionally competent in many things. He built gates and picket fences for us and helped around the farm on other work when the spirit moved him. Generally, he chose his own work and no one seemed to mind. Since he didn't go to church, he was pleased to look after our autistic son, Elvin, on Sunday mornings. That was a real contribution.

He had a family. In fact, probably several. But his relaxed views about responsibility for wives and children had alien-

Ada Marie, Catherine, and I ready for church in 1947.

ated him from any family members. That's the reason he was homeless at an age when he needed care. And he had this thirst problem.

Ordinarily, it was no problem because we didn't have alcohol and he had no money. But he received a very small monthly pension of some sort. When the check arrived, he would go to town for a day or two. He could drink a pint of whiskey in a short while and still walk reasonably straight.

But gradually, he lost his ability to carry his liquor. Then his return to our home would be awkward. I tried to lay down the law—if he wanted to go drinking, he had to make up his own mind, but if he went he could not return.

The pressure was too great after a while and he would go. Then he would be sorry, ask forgiveness, and promise to do better. It went on for over four years until I finally told him, "No more!" It lasted a while but he relapsed again. This time I didn't take him back. It was painful because we had come to accept him more or less as family. When he sobered up, he was both destitute and homeless. His last years were spent in the Pocopsin Home in Chester County. Shortly before his death he requested baptism. I was privileged to be there when bishop Kready performed the ceremony.

18.

Life
in the
1950s

My Trip to Europe and the Holy Lands

On October 22, 1951, my brother-in-law, Tobe Bontrager, and I joined a large tour group for a trip to Europe and the Holy Lands. The voyage across the ocean on the Queen Mary was a memorable experience with very good food. This ship was nearly 1,000 feet long. I had the idea that a ship as long as this wouldn't be affected much by a storm.

The second day out we ran into a 100-mph wind. Or it ran into us. I spent most of that day in my bunk. It just wasn't fit to walk around. Everyone staggered around as the ship tossed drunkenly. We watched the wild waves through the portholes. When the ship rocked, the dishes slid off the table. The waiters put up little sideboards to keep things from leaving the table for the floor. Not many people made it to the dining room for a while.

The motion did some interesting things to the insides. For a lot of people, it seemed there was a storm with its own

The Cunard Queen Elizabeth. In October 1951, I joined a tour group for a trip to Europe and the Holy Lands. We sailed to Europe on the Queen Mary and returned on the Queen Elizabeth.

waves inside their insides. Tobe was very seasick. Somehow I managed not to get sick in spite of Anna's observation before the trip that I wouldn't be on the ship long until I would be feeding my dentures to the fish. The huge ship groaned and creaked, but it sailed right on through the storm. Smaller vessels would have had to turn and ride it out.

We spent several days in England, then crossed the North Sea for Holland at night. In Holland we visited a Dutch Mennonite church and were impressed with the farms whose economy seemed to be built on cows and tulips. Canals surrounded pastures blanketed by black and white cows. Cows sometimes rode to pasture on canal boats.

Driving through Germany in 1951, one still saw lots of damage from the war. Most bridges along the Rhine River were bombed out. We crossed the Rhine by ferry on the way to Frankfurt. I took several days on my own and spent some time visiting German Mennonite farmers. I saw how land had been divided and subdivided through the years because of inheritances. One farm which I visited had 50 acres in 34 different plots. It seemed to me that lots of space was wasted in field lanes.

Here is proof that a "Camel Walked a Mile" for me. I am in the back row on the right of the photo.

Our group traveled on to Switzerland and Italy. From Rome, we flew to Egypt where we went for a tourist-style camel ride to the pyramids.

Along the way, we frequently had problems at the borders because we were crossing into Arab countries. The guards were often certain that my name, Aaron Stephen Glick, must be Jewish. We spent time in Amman and in Jericho before heading for Jerusalem. For me, it was a moving experience to be in the land where Jesus walked, lived, and taught. I especially noticed how much of the land in Israel was being reforested, making it more productive. I remembered the Old Testament prophecy, "The wilderness and the solitary place shall rejoice, and the desert shall blossom like a rose."

From Jerusalem, we flew to Greece and back to Rome. We traveled through Italy by bus to Lyon, France, and on to Paris. There we said goodbye to our tour group. After the six most interesting weeks in my life, Tobe Bontrager and I spent several more weeks in Europe. We decided to fly into the bombed-out city of Berlin.

While in Berlin, we stayed at the Mennonite Central Committee Relief Center. Hiram Hershey from Lansdale,

(top) Bombed-out Berlin as it looked when my brother-in-law, Tobe Bontrager, and I visited in 1951, several years after the end of World War II.

(bottom) A warning sign on the border between East and West Berlin in 1951.

Pennsylvania, was living there, doing a term of 1-W service (the draft classification given to concientious objectors). Hiram took us to the Eastern sector past the Russian border guards. The guards paid little attention to us as we walked by. Because of our dialect and our plain Amish clothes, Hiram thought the border guards may have mistaken us for peasants or refugees. In East Berlin, we noticed that everyone in the crowds seemed to look at our shoes. Shoes were rationed in the East Zone and anyone with new shoes must be from the West Zone.

We purchased the souvenirs that had been our excuse for crossing over and returned to the American sector. We walked by the Russian border guards without difficulty. They stopped and checked all the cars but, to our relief, did not bother with us.

On our walk into the Russian sector of East Berlin, we had been taken for refugees because of our dialect. On the flight out of Berlin, my German seatmate took me for a Hungarian. He imagined I was probably a Hungarian wine merchant. It didn't occur to him that Tobe and I might be Amish-Americans, as the Germans called us.

We spent a day in Luxembourg and then went to the Alsace Lorraine area of France where we again had trouble at the border. It seemed that because we visited so many countries in such a short time and had our passports stamped everytime, as was the rule right after the war, they felt we must be smugglers. We finally made it through the border and spent a rewarding day with the Hege family near Strasbourg, France.

Anna and I had become acquainted with the Heges when their son, Fritz, stayed in our home under the Mennonite Central Committee trainee program. From the Alsace, we took an overnight train to Paris and on to Cherbourg on the coast where we boarded the Queen Elizabeth for our trip home. Because of fog, the ship was delayed from evening until two in the morning. It was several days before Christmas and we were on the ocean again. Tobe Bontrager was seasick again. He said he might as well be seasick if he couldn't be with his family for Christmas anyway.

Europe's Displaced Persons

They came to us in the 1950s. By the end of World War II, hundreds of thousands of displaced persons found themselves in Germany and Austria. Some were brought into Germany as forced laborers. Others fled west from Eastern-bloc countries as the Soviets fought their way westward. And many ethnic Germans in what had been eastern Germany had to make room for the Poles who were shoved westward when the Soviets annexed eastern Poland. Whole populations were uprooted. Generally, the refugees were well ahead of the retreating German army on the trek west. They tried to make sure they were winning that race. Losers faced Soviet prison camps or worse.

Relief agencies tried to help. The Mennonite Central Committee tried to provide assistance to those who stayed in Europe while the Brethren Service Committee was more active in bringing refugees to the United States.

Immigration laws were fairly strict. In addition to health requirements, each refugee had to have a sponsor—someone who would guarantee that the new immigrant would never become a burden on the government. If you sponsored a refugee, you were literally responsible for that person till death! Not many people volunteered for the opportunity.

Anna and I decided to trust the Lord for the future. In the short run, we realized that we could help and, therefore, we should. Many of the displaced persons who came to us quickly discovered families. That is why a substantial number of people stayed with us only briefly. The Maerz family was a notable exception. An ethnic German family of ten, they settled into Lancaster County life and have made many contributions to the community.

✦ ✦ ✦

Then there was Simon Prociw with his wife Fronie and a young daughter. They had met and married in a refugee camp in Europe. Simon, whose home was in the Ukraine, had been a forced laborer in Germany. He was captured one Sunday morning while attending mass. The Germans surrounded the church during the service and took all the men along. Simon never returned to his home from church. Instead he came to us.

Like the others, he and Fronie brought little with them except some nondescript clothing in a wooden box that had been an army shell case. They stayed with us for seven years, living in an apartment above our broiler house on the Brook farm.

By then he had saved some money because they lived very simply. We had to find other work for him after 1953 when the collapse of the beef market nearly put us out of business and we could no longer pay him. But they stayed on the Brook farm and helped with the chores instead of paying rent. That's how it came to be that he and his wife were able to build a new, brick ranch-style house on a lot we sold them. They filled it with new furniture and paid for the house and furniture in cash. In just seven years!

For the first years, Simon and Fronie didn't have a car. He worked for Jonas and Amos Zook as a carpenter, and they always stopped by to pick him up.

Once, in the middle of winter, they were framing a new house. The weather was bitter and Simon was chilled and got sick. His eyes watered and nearly swelled shut. But miserable as he was, he had to wait for his ride home in the evening. By then he was looking so miserable that the other carpenters started to tease him about it. So Simon said, "All right. Today you laughing. Tomorrow I laughing." That was the cause for even more amusement on the part of the other men.

At home that evening, he sat down with a handful of garlic bulbs. A whole bunch, really. One by one, he chewed the garlic cloves down. He used some bread to sort of push them down. After he had swallowed a cupful or more of the raw garlic, he went to bed.

The next morning his cold and illness were gone. The swelling was gone from his face. His eyes weren't watering and his sinuses had cleared. He could breathe. The driver, Jonas Zook, drove up to pick him up for work. The windows were closed and the pickup's heater was going full blast because of the severe cold. Simon got in and Jonas put the pickup in reverse to back out of the driveway. But he quickly stopped the pickup, cranked down the window, and put his head out to gasp for air. The wall of garlic odor had hit him full force. Simon was ready. "Whatsa matter? You too many hot?" he asked. Then he added, "I said, today you laughing, tomorrow I laughing."

Simon has been an affectionate neighbor. Fronie has gone to her reward, but Simon is still with us almost 40 years after coming to America.

The 1950s also marked our involvement with the Mennonite Central Committee's Farm Youth Exchange Program. Young men from Germany, France, and Paraguay lived with us for six-month periods. This was an excellent learning experience for us. Friendships were formed that remain precious and active 40 years later.

My Ordination to the Ministry in 1953

At the time of the 1953 Sunday school reorganization in our Beachy Amish congregation, I was elected to teach the men's class. Sometime during the early fall of that year, I was told of plans for ordination of a minister at Weavertown. The first news of this was a real shock to me.

The thought of the coming ordination continued to preoccupy me in spite of an effort to dismiss it. I felt like the Psalmist in 32:4, "For day and night thy hand was heavy upon me." Finally the day of the ordination arrived. This was an exciting day of anticipation for the Weavertown congregation. Several visiting ministers were with us, including Jake Hershberger from Norfolk, Virginia.

The votes were taken in the morning near the close of the regular service. By that time I was reconciled to accepting the call to the ministry if the Lord so chose. When the names of those who had three or more votes (only those with three votes or more were in the class for the lot) were read, my name was given as the last one. The others in the lot were Christ Beiler, Christ Kauffman, John Yoder, Amos Zook,

Ervin Miller, Ben B. Beiler, Aaron Beiler, and Ben Lapp. On the way home from the service that morning, my wife Anna said, "Now I know why the Lord spoke to me last night." What she told me verified my feeling that I was being called into the ministry.

That afternoon all of us in the class met with the ministers because there were things that needed to be discussed with each of us before the ordination that evening. In the evening the worship service was held at the church and, near the close of the service, nine identical hymn books were placed on the table in front of the pulpit. In one of the books there was a paper indicating that the individual who took this book was being chosen by the Lord for the ministry. The paper had been put in the book by one of the visiting ministers in the basement of the church, and a little later another individual was made responsible to shuffle the books and bring them up and place them on the table. Only the Lord knew in which book the paper would be found.

After prayer, asking the Lord to direct, we were instructed to each take a book. As I was the oldest in the class I went first. There were nine books to choose from. I was definitely moved to take the first book; I could not have taken any other. After each had taken a book, the bishop proceeded to examine the books and found the paper in my book. I was asked to kneel, and bishop John A. Stoltzfus ordained me to the ministry by the laying on of his hands, with the charge of pastor and teacher, a lifetime calling.

After the suspense and the ordination, there were many well-wishing friends who greeted me, wishing the Lord's blessing for me in the work I was now called to.

After the ordination, I realized I was somewhat like a sailor on a voyage without a chart. I needed help. So I contacted my friend, evangelist Andrew Jantzi, for advice. He stated one thing very emphatically, "Aaron, above all things always be kind, in every situation you meet." I soon learned the value of his advice. To acquire a fuller working knowledge of the Bible, I also attended evening Bible classes at Lancaster School of the Bible midwinter term for a number of years.

The first years I was in the ministry, services were still conducted in German, but after I had spent about 15 years preaching in the dialect, our group decided to adopt the English language for church services.

In addition to the work of the ministry at home, I was called to church-related duties in the many widely scattered Beachy Amish congregations in other states. This consisted of Bible doctrinal teaching, as well as teaching at our youth Winter Bible School at Calico Rock, Arkansas, and visiting and counseling our younger brethren in 1-W service. I was also asked to teach in Bible study groups in the home community. This was mostly among those Old Order Amish folks who later organized the Amish New Order Group in 1967.

Two members of this group, Christ Lapp and Bennie Stoltzfus, contacted me in 1965 and asked me to lead in their Bible study. At first I declined, thinking this would surely give them problems with their Old Order Amish church elders. But they said there was no need to be concerned because they were eager for Bible study. This midweek Bible study and time of sharing, as well as the others with whom I met biweekly, was a source of real inspiration. There were seven groups, many of whom had not had previous opportunity for organized Bible study. Many people from these groups eventually either became New Order Amish or joined one of the Beachy Amish churches in Lancaster County. Several of the men later were also ordained to the ministry.

The Founding of the Pequea Beachy Amish Church

The Pequea congregation was established as a result of the Weavertown church over-filling. There were 46 classes in Sunday school in 1959. The local grange hall was rented in 1960 for Sunday school to relieve the crowded condition at Weavertown until other arrangements could be made.

In late 1961, land for the Pequea church building was purchased from the Henry Lapp farm a half mile west of Cains along Route 340. The first Sunday school held at Pequea was on February 18, 1962. The first regular church service was held there July 1, 1962. The ministers of

Weavertown all rotated to Pequea until September 1969. At that time, I was appointed to minister at Pequea until deacon Jonathan S. Stoltzfus was ordained as bishop. On March 25, 1979, Jonathan was ordained to have charge of the ministry there.

My Trip to Red Lake, Ontario, in 1956

In September of 1956, I was invited to join several other men from the Weavertown church for a trip to Red Lake, Ontario. We would be helping to build a school with Northern Light Gospel Mission, a work which was being led by Ervin Shantz. The Weavertown brethren who made that trip included Sim Kauffman, Ben B. Beiler, Henry Lapp, and Will Stoltzfus. We traveled in Sim Kauffman's car with Ben B. Beiler sharing the driving. We pulled a trailer with supplies for the Red Lake mission.

Our first day out, we had a flat tire on the trailer, so we parked and several of us stayed with the trailer while the others went to get another tire. The next morning we continued toward Red Lake. I remember we stopped at a trading post in the north country, probably for gas. The woman in charge asked us who we were, and why we dressed like we did. I asked her about her religious affiliation. She said they were Lutherans. She agreed that the Bible does teach modesty in dress. I observed that Lutherans allow the individual to make the decision as to what is modest, while we decide our dress as a group. She seemed to be satisfied with my answer.

We arrived at Red Lake late in the evening, having crossed a stream by ferry. We stayed at the mission headquarters overnight. The next day Ervin Shantz flew us to Pikangikum, where we would be working. There was no road.

We worked together with the Voluntary Service (VS) unit for about ten days. The VS team included David and Elva Burkholder, as well as Arthur and Lavina Kauffman. It was there that I first preached a funeral sermon. It was for an Indian baby.

There is something about the north woods that is refresh-

The school which I helped build in Pikangikum in the Red Lake region of Ontario. Five men from the Weavertown congregation made the 1956 trip to offer our services in building the school.

ingly invigorating. The air and the moose meat diet were a part of it. Perhaps the Spaniard, Ponce de Leon, should have gone to the north woods instead of Florida to find the Fountain of Youth.

They took us out to an island in the lake by canoe and parked us there every morning. One of our group jokingly remarked that this was like the island prison Alcatraz where one had to stay. Arthur Kauffman used to bring our lunch by canoe every noon. In my mind's eye I can still see him coming across the lake in the distance. The logs were floated across the lake for the building.

We had decided to travel home by way of Kalona, Iowa. We left Red Lake in the evening and failed to fill up with gas at the last station open along the way. The stations were few and far between. We intended to drive all night, but you can't drive without gas. At a very late hour we came to another outpost, but it was closed.

There in the middle of the north country they didn't have night fuel service, but we needed gas. After much effort we were able to locate the postmaster, already in bed. He made contact for us with the filling station operator, who got out of bed to serve us. We got our breakfast in Minnesota and

The 180 Cessna on floats. Ervin Shantz flew us from Red Lake to Pikangikum in this plane.

arrived at Sharon Center south of Iowa City in time for supper at the home of Ralph and Martha Schlabach. Martha was Anna's sister. They had been expecting us and were prepared with a good Iowa meal.

In the morning we went to Kalona. We spent the rest of the day visiting friends. We attended midweek worship with the Conservative group, where our friend Elmer Swartzentruber was in charge. After the Wednesday evening meeting, we decided to start for home right away. Driving all night, we switched drivers, making sure someone always stayed awake with the driver.

The next forenoon it was nice and sunny. We were traveling along, and one by one each of us on the back seat fell asleep. Finally the one in the front beside the driver dozed off; then our driver fell asleep, too.

I remember waking up to a banging noise, something like tin cans crashing together. We had just sideswiped a car that had been traveling in the opposite direction. So instead of running into a pole, the Lord spared our lives by having a car meet us. The only damage was some peeled off chrome. The other driver had seen that our car was gradually crossing the center line and had feared for his life. He was shaking like a leaf. We had acted foolishly by driving without ade-

Our daughters, Ada Marie (left) and Kathy (right) taking a buggy ride with a friend during the 1950s.

quate rest. My father's brother, Uncle Chriss, the Montana homesteader, used to say, "The Lord takes care of fools and little children." In this case, I guess he was right.

PART FOUR:
THE 1960s
AND BEYOND

19.

A Beachy Amish Alternate Service Program

In the early '60s I was appointed, along with several other Beachy Amish ministers, to help oversee a Beachy Amish Alternate Service program similar to the Civilian Public Service of World War II.

During the years of World War II, provisions had been made by the U.S. government for conscientious objectors to work in alternate service programs so they would not need to serve in the armed forces or go to prison, as had been the case in World War I. Work deemed of national importance—such as work in both regular and mental hospitals, forestry work and dairy testing, and, in some cases, even work on dairy farms—was provided.

There were concientious objector (CO) camps in different parts of the nation where many of the draftees stayed. From the base camps, they were sent to their job assignments. After the war, the camps were closed. But all young men were still required to register for the draft when they reached the age of 18.

For several years after World War II, there were no calls from the draft boards. The army made do with volunteers for replacements. Then in the early 1960s, at the beginning of the Vietnam War, the draft was resumed. This time there were no camps for the conscientious objectors.

When the draft was resumed in 1960, the Beachy churches made a unified attempt to provide orientation and counseling for the young men drafted into 1-W service (1-W was defined as Class 1 Work). For the most part, they served in hospitals and related jobs such as children's and convalescent homes. Some found jobs with other U.S. government-approved programs. But the environment at some locations and the involvement in recreational activities with local workers had an unfortunate effect on some of the young men. Having grown up in a sheltered society, they were rubbing shoulders with "the world." The results left lifelong scars on the lives of several who were not prepared to cope with an environment radically different from that in which they had been nurtured. Hence, the church felt a need to provide support for the young men.

By 1961, the Beachy 1-W support program embraced 30 Beachy Amish congregations across the country. They were divided into four districts—the Eastern (Seaboard) District, the Ohio and Western Pennsylvania District, the Indiana and Illinois District, and the Western District, which included the two midwestern states of Oklahoma and Kansas.

A counselor was assigned to each district to make occasional visits to those in service, "to sit where they sit" (Ezekiel 3:15), and to empathize with them. I was appointed counselor for the Eastern District, which included the eastern seaboard all the way to Miami, Florida. All those in service who desired it were to be interviewed, regardless of church affiliation. The staff was included if they so desired. This was usually a very rich, heartwarming experience.

The ways in which the young brethren served their 1-W service differed. Those serving at the Beltsville, Maryland, United States Department of Agriculture (USDA) research farm were responsible for their own lodging and meals. At

Beltsville, the young men were paid wages. This was also true at the various hospitals in Maryland and Pennsylvania where the men worked.

In other places, the COs worked without pay, receiving food and lodging instead. These places included the Sunnyside Old People's Home in Sarasota, Florida; Mountain View Old People's Home in Virginia; and the Faith Mission Children's Home also in Virginia. At Fellowship Haven in Washington DC, the 1-Ws were about equally divided between voluntary and wage-earning service.

Not all of the young men were always eager for my visit. In fact, there were sometimes occasions when particular individuals arranged to be absent if they knew I was going to be there.

I found it a pleasure to accept the offer of Dan King (a Beachy Amish preacher from Belleville, Pennsylvania) to provide transportation for me and to share in the visits with those 1-W workers in the hospitals on the Maryland side of Washington DC. Sometimes our efforts included placing young men.

On one of our trips, we attended a meeting with Major General Lewis Hershey at the Continental Hotel in Washington DC. He was meeting with a group from the National Service Board for Religious Objectors (NSBRO). General Hershey was in charge of Selective Service—the draft. At the meeting, several religious objectors were very vocal in their objection to the draft. This seemed inappropriate to our Amish orientation. We preferred quiet accommodation within the framework of freedom of conscience.

When we left there, in gathering up our luggage, we mistakenly included a briefcase that was not ours, but without name. It was the overnight bag of a U.S. Senator's assistant. Dan King was able to see to the return of the person's property. But, as I recall, he would have been without his pajamas and razor for a while.

Through the years, I traveled many miles with Dan King for matters that concerned the business part of the 1-W program. At the annual Beachy minister's meeting, he always explained the progress and direction of the program. His report usually

My grandchildren, Susan and Douglas, playing near the 1951 Ford convertible which I drove from Lancaster to St. Louis for their parents—Ada Marie and Truman Mast—in 1963.

began with "Hitherto hath the Lord helped us."

There were various other church-related activities during the 1960s that required much time and study. I was asked to teach the book of Revelation at midweek meetings at the Rohrerstown Mennonite Church. The first time I was called to conduct a series of revival meetings was in the Buffalo Valley area of Pennsylvania in 1962, at the Buffalo Valley

Crossroads Church. Rudy Byler was pastor there at that time. This group later developed into the Shady Grove congregation where David King now has pastoral oversight.

The greatest challenge in all the years of my ministry came when I was asked to preach a funeral sermon in a Catholic church. Imagine, an Amish minister preaching in a Catholic funeral service!

The occasion arose when a young man, a relative of our family, was killed in a truck accident. Many of his friends who seldom attended worship services of any sort attended the funeral. My text was taken from the Prophet Amos, Chapter 4, verse 12, "Prepare to meet thy God." I appreciated the privilege of having part in that service, and the blessing experienced through it.

✦ ✦ ✦

By this time our daughter, Ada Marie, had married Dr. Truman Mast. In 1963, they were living in St. Louis and Truman asked me to bring them a car he had purchased. It was a restored 1951 Ford convertible, black with white sidewall tires.

On my way, I stopped over with the Beachy Woodlawn congregation near Goshen, Indiana, for weekend meetings. I also stopped over in Kalona, Iowa, to visit my brother-in-law Tobe Bontrager, who was quite ill at the time. From Iowa, I headed to St. Louis.

On the first day's drive, the car's cloth top was ripped open by the strong April wind, and it was too cold to drive without the top. So I had to stop for a new top. Yes, buying a convertible top was a pretty unusual activity for a Beachy Amish preacher!

20.

How We
Made Our Living
in the 1960s

After we sold the two neighboring farms which we had purchased during the 1950s, I decided I should have a part-time job off the farm, since Ivan was quite capable of taking care of the home farm workload. And we needed the income. We had not yet generated enough income to pay the large debt that faced us, thanks to our failed steer feeding effort in the early 1950s.

My brother Jacob gave me part-time employment at Glick's Plant Farm for the spring and early summer of 1961. In the fall I helped with my brother Daniel's tomato enterprise.

The next year (1962) and the years following, I worked at Glick's Plant Farm most of the time when I was not occupied with church-related work. I prepared and mixed the soil and filled the flats. The transplanters then planted vegetable and flower seedlings for the early spring trade. This required the filling of thousands of flats. This work was all done in the stable of the old barn on my father's original Smoketown farm. The barn burned down in 1963, and we had to move our transplanting operation to a different building.

During those years, I was given the responsibility to plant farm crops on the acres not needed to grow vegetable and flowering plants. There was seed wheat for Rohrer's Seed company, corn for grain, and Hubbard squash for Consumer Packing Company of Lancaster. The heavy squash were loaded with pitchforks. There were many truckloads. Some of that land is now the asphalt runway of the Smoketown airport operated by my nephew, Melvin, and his son-in-law, Doug Fretz.

21.

PAX, MCC, and Cows for Crete

Lyndon Johnson was still our president in 1966. At Christmas there was a 48-hour truce in Vietnam. Many of us found it hard to understand why the killing had to resume again if it could be put off for 48 hours. Surely, a longer, permanent procrastination should be equally possible.

In those years, scientists made some new discoveries. An artificial, plastic heart was first implanted in a person in 1966. The patient lived a couple of weeks. An unmanned American spaceship landed on the moon and sent back a lot of pictures. But from my viewpoint, the most important thing about 1966 was the chance to be a flying cowboy on an airplane load of animals destined for the island of Crete.

A number of American Mennonite PAX men were working on Crete. It was an alternative to military service, but they had to sign up for three years, not two, and they were unpaid volunteers. As part of their job on the island, they were doing agricultural development work in cooperation with the Greek

Orthodox bishop. The bishop had a farm and school for orphan boys.

Coming from high-tech American farms, the Mennonite PAX men were not at all impressed by the quality of the livestock they found on Crete. One thing led to another and their friends back home decided to contribute some better animals for breeding to improve the livestock farms on the island.

The Mennonite Central Committee was asked to coordinate the PAX effort. The paperwork for shipment would be handled by the Brethren Service Committee's Heifer Project at New Windsor, Maryland. The air freight would be paid by the U.S. Government.

But MCC needed someone to do the detail work here. They called my son Ivan and asked him to look after it. That came about because he had been active in getting flour mills, farm machinery, seeds, and other things to Paraguay and elsewhere in support of MCC projects. Of course he agreed.

When he hung up the phone from that conversation, he called me first thing and told me to get my passport renewed and to decide who should go with me. The person that would go with me to help take care of the livestock on the way to Crete should be the man I felt would most benefit from having his "windows opened" for a broader outlook.

Ivan wanted to go but couldn't because he had a full-time job off the farm in addition to the farm, and he needed all available vacation time for farm work. Things were improving for us, but we were still deeply in debt. He was tied down and had to stay home. I was free to go.

Crete was one of the places I was eager to visit. I had always been interested in ancient history, and the history of Crete is about as ancient as it gets. Furthermore, our youngest daughter, Kathy, was teaching in a girls' school in Tanzania. I decided that from Crete the distance was not too great, and I would be able to visit her as well.

A well-known Pennsylvania Holstein breeder, Alpheus Ruth, offered to contribute a bull of superior genetics to the project. Others contributed purebred heifers. Purebred breeding units of several breeds of hogs were rounded up, but we needed more heifers.

That's how it happened a letter went to the Beachy Amish churches on May 27, 1966, explaining the project and the need for a number of purebred heifers—yearlings or two-year-olds. The response was immediate, just as it would be today. In a short time, we had as many heifers, all top quality, as we needed.

Meanwhile, there was a lot of work. It turned out that every single animal had to have its own government-approved health examination and documents. Nevermind that the animals were being contributed, not sold. The place of assembly would have to be steam-cleaned and disinfected to make sure they remained unexposed to disease until shipment. Then when a government veterinarian had checked it all out and verified that every piece of paper for every animal was in perfect order, the animals could be loaded on disinfected trucks, sealed with a government seal, and transported to the airport.

I left the details to Ivan who handled them as best he could. Paul Smucker offered his new barn as a place where the animals could be gathered. Since no animals had yet been put into his barn, it was approved without the costly cleaning and disinfecting.

Some of the animals were delivered to the Smucker farm. Others Ivan had to pick up. The bull was on a farm over 50 miles away. To get him, Ivan borrowed a truck from his brother-in-law in the evening after work and made the trip. By the time he got back to Paul Smucker's barn, it was the middle of the night with no one in sight. After worrying about it on the way home, he figured out how to get the bull off safely.

He backed up to the barn, tied one end of a long rope to the bull's ring and looped the other end around a post inside the barn. That way he would be able to control the animal and not be in danger of being gored. Then he untied the bull on the truck and guided him into the barn by pulling on the other end of the rope. The bull wasn't all that pleased, but

John Blank looks on while the veterinarian checks the papers for a load of cows and pigs to Crete. David Miller, Thomas, Oklahoma, and I escorted the animals to Crete.

he had to cooperate and, next thing he knew, found himself tied to the post in the Smucker barn.

Finally, all the animals were on hand. I think Ivan made at least one last-minute trip to Harrisburg for a missing health document for one heifer. We were worried that the government veterinary inspector would find something to gripe about and hold up the entire shipment. We needn't have worried. When he came and looked things over and had put his seal on the trucks, he commented that he had never handled a shipment where all the papers were in such good order.

The shipment included twelve heifers, one bull, and twenty pigs, all registered breeding stock. Local heifer con-

Loading pigs onto a plane bound for Crete on the tarmac at Kennedy International Airport in New York.

tributors included George Beiler, Calvin Beiler, Reuben Smoker, Allen Lee Stoltzfus, Ivan Zook, Gideon Stoltzfus of Atglen, and Christian Yoder of Grantsville. The others were sent by the families and friends of the PAX men in Ohio and the midwest. I decided to ask bishop David Miller from the Beachy Amish congregation in Thomas, Oklahoma, to be my traveling companion.

217

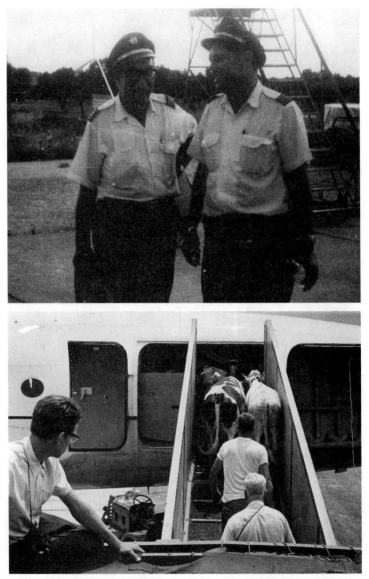

(top) Our pilots for the flight to Crete. They were veterans of the Bay of Pigs operation.

(bottom) Loading the heifers.

A Holstein passenger checks in for assigned seating. That's Amos Stoltzfus and Gid Stoltzfus in the background.

After the animals were loaded onto a disinfected truck and sealed with the federal seal, they were trucked to Kennedy International Airport in New York City, an overnight run. A group of our folks took David Miller and me to the airport early on the morning of June 23. At 7 AM, the plane had not yet arrived.

When it finally arrived, it was a rickety looking sort of flying boxcar. A converted four-motor, propeller-type passenger plane, it had a door in the side like a barn door, not too tightly fitted, and it also had some bullet holes. Our folks who had gone along to help load the heifers were not enthused to have two of their ministers leave for a transatlantic flight in such an old tub.

The pilots were Spanish-speaking Cubans. Apparently, they and their machine had been in the Bay of Pigs action in 1963. Now they were providing nonscheduled air transport. The seats of the plane had been removed, except for two in the tail section. Four pens were made for the cattle by placing gates crosswise in the plane directly behind the pilots. So position wise, the heifers were traveling first class, the pigs second class, and my colleague and I back in the tail of the plane were clearly in third class.

The temperature on that day was nearly 100 degrees Fahrenheit at the airport. Before we took off, one of the pilots remarked that it might get quite cold in the plane when we were up in the air. Suddenly we realized that we weren't prepared for cold. We didn't know how much cold air would blow in beside the door and through the bullet holes. Sam Lapp gave us a comforter. Amos Stoltzfus gave me his coveralls. I also put on all the other clothes that I had. But we were still very cold. The temperature was near or below freezing on the flight to St. Johns, Newfoundland, our first stop.

The heifers and the pigs seemed to fare better than we did. We found that cowboy life in the air was not exactly comfortable. We landed at Newfoundland around 8:30 that evening. After a lot of effort, we were able to borrow two parkas and a blanket-lined long coat with a hood. Then we were able to stay warm. We made another stop in the Azores Islands where we watered the livestock. The water was provided by native help with a long firehose. At the Azores we were able to get a good dinner at the airport restaurant. By that time we were hungry.

From the Azores we flew to Madrid. The folks there were excited and anxious to see our planeload of livestock. I would benefit from this publicity later in the day in an adventure occasioned by a misunderstanding.

The pilot informed us that the plane needed repair. And the next day we would fly nonstop to Crete. It is possible he only wanted a free night in Madrid. At any rate, the airplane clearly didn't seem to be in the best of shape, and you'd like it to be fixed up pretty good if you're going along. So they parked the plane with its heifers near the end of the runway. There we settled for the night.

As I thought of the next day's flight and the meager box lunch that we were getting in flight, I suggested to David that we walk back to the airport restaurant and buy some oranges

An international traveler gets her first look at Crete.

for the next day. He agreed but soon went back to the plane and fell asleep.

I walked quite a distance on the runway until I finally saw some lights in a building. Entering it I found a snack bar. But they didn't have oranges and spoke neither English nor German. So after leaving the snack bar, I saw a parked panel truck with several men eating their lunch. I tried talking with them, but without success. They spoke only Spanish.

As I was walking back toward the plane, I was approached by a man in uniform who said something in Spanish as I was passing by. I didn't pay attention and he spoke louder. I didn't understand a word he was saying. When he grabbed me by the shoulder, he got my attention. This was at the time Castro was making confusion in Cuba and it is possible

(top) Unloading the livestock on Crete. Dave Miller from Thomas, Oklahoma, is inside the plane. I am setting up a rail to guide the cattle safely from the plane to a dump truck. From the dump truck, we loaded them into a cattle truck and took them to their destination.

that because of my beard he might have suspected me to be a stowaway from Cuba. Since the officer spoke only Spanish and I was rather anxious that he let me go, I was able to explain to him in signs and wonders—he did the wondering—that I was with the planeload of livestock parked down the runway. As soon as I was able to get that message through, he let me go on. I had to return to the plane empty-handed. Meanwhile Dave Miller had slept through all the fun.

When we finally arrived on Crete, we were faced with the problem of unloading the animals. The plane was high off the ground, and there was no loading chute. A man came out with a forklift. The local folks had a few ideas that seemed quite impractical to me. They wanted to use a cart like those used to haul suitcases and lift it with a forklift. Their suggestion was to lead the heifers out onto the cart and let them down one by one. I refused. I was afraid the heifers would jump or fall off.

I requested a high dump truck which they soon brought. I used planks to make a ramp. From the dump truck, we

(left to right) Aaron Glick, the Orthodox Metropolitan of Crete (the chief bishop on the island), David Miller, and the local priest, who gave us beds in his home while we were on the island.

led them down another ramp into a cattle truck. We met with the PAX men at their unit house and afterwards went to the house of the local Orthodox priest where we stayed for the night.

From Crete we flew to Athens and on to Beirut, Lebanon. We stayed in Beirut overnight and got an afternoon flight to Jerusalem where we spent several days.

I cautioned David Miller not to drink water unless it was boiled. But during the heat of the day, he was thirsty. There was a vendor with a large can on his shoulder selling homemade root beer. Thirsty, David bought some. The vendor had only one drinking cup for all his customers. Afterwards he rinsed out the cup with his hand and poured the rinse water back into a container for reuse for the next customer. Water in the old city was a scarce commodity. The next morning David was very sick with the old ailment

On my trip to the Holy Lands with David Miller, we stopped at the site where Moses smote the rock during the exodus. That's me on the right.

peculiar to tourists. In Mexico they call it Montezuma's Revenge. It takes the joy out of living for a while.

After David's intestinal distress had played itself out, we decided to go to Petra for a day. We stopped at Mt. Nebo where Moses stood to view the promised land. Along the way we came to Moses' Rock where water now gushes forth from a six-inch pipe. It was very good water and safe to drink. I put some in a bottle to take along home.

We entered Petra on horseback, then walked up through cliffs nearly three miles to the top of the mountain. From there we could see Mt. Sinai in the distance. Walking time was about three hours.

When we returned, we rode our horses over the old Roman pavement, and after lunch, headed back to Jerusalem, arriving there about eleven at night. The restaurant at the YWCA where we were staying had already closed. The only drinking water available was chlorinated faucet water. David was very thirsty because he had been sick the day before and had lost a lot of fluid. He lamented, if only he had some good Oklahoma water. So I gave him a glass of the Moses water I had brought along from the Rock. He smacked his lips and would have downed it all, but I hid the rest of the water so his thirst wouldn't get the best of him during the night when I was sleeping. Unfortunately, the water all leaked out of the bottle, and I didn't have any Moses water left anyway by the time I got home.

We went on to Tel Aviv where we found lodging in a private home. We waited at the bus station for two of David Miller's friends to take us on a tour. They were Ken Bailey from Oklahoma and Ervin Bontrager from Indiana. These young men were doing a term of Voluntary Service on a farm kibbutz near Tel Aviv with others from Holland and Switzerland. It was an international group, working together, dedicated to improving working relations between Christians and Jews. The name of the kibbutz was Nes Aminm.

Ken and Ervin spent several days with us, taking us to various points of interest. In the cities of Haifa and Tel Aviv, we met multitudes of Jews from many countries. Many were European and spoke Yiddish, which is similar to our Pennsylvania Dutch dialect, so we could converse freely.

✦ ✦ ✦

After our ten-day tour of the Middle East, we headed for our next destination—Dodoma, Tanzania, where my daughter Kathy was teaching in a church school. When we landed at Addis Ababa, Ethiopia, we had missed our flight to Kenya. We found hotel accommodations for the night at the airline's expense. At lunch time we went to the dining room. But they wouldn't let us in to eat because we didn't wear neckties. We were told our meal would be sent to our rooms. We waited and waited for our lunch, but none came.

Finally I said to David, "Let's go see about getting lunch."

My certificate from Ethiopian Airlines, registering the fact that I had flown across the Equator.

I told the hotel clerk why they wouldn't let us into the dining room to eat. So that he would understand, I explained that we were priests of our religion and our priests didn't wear ties. Then we were permitted into their elegant dining room to eat. I hadn't planned to tell this at home, but Dave found the joke too good to keep.

We were able to secure a flight to Nairobi the next morning where we were met by Hershey Leaman, a former neighbor boy, who was in charge of the mission unit there. We spent the day at a game reserve, then took a bus to Arusha, Uganda, and on to Dodoma in Tanzania. The drive through the night was through lion country. But no lions came to help us push the bus.

The driver had to slow down several times to let giraffes cross the road. They seemed to have the right-of-way. Riding along we observed villages of huts with grass-covered roofs. These villages were completely surrounded by a thorny hedge about ten feet high to keep the wild animals out. On the return trip, we saw several lions feasting on a giraffe carcass along the way.

The bus that was to take us to Dodoma, a distance of nearly 300 miles, had already left when we arrived at Arusha. And no bus was due until the next day. I didn't fancy staying there overnight, and hitchhiking was suggested as a solution. I couldn't imagine hitchhiking through lion country.

I decided to go to the local bank for advice, as the banker can usually be relied upon. We were well advised by the banker and were able to find a person with a pickup truck who took us to Dodoma in Tanzania. Along the way, we stopped for fruit. Several men of the Masai tribe arranged with our driver to ride with us to another village quite a distance away.

We arrived in Dodoma in the evening and met my daughter Kathy and a friend of hers, Margaret Walker, an Australian teacher. The cottages at the school where they were teaching were quite modern. We were assigned a nice cottage, and after a good supper, we were ready for a good night's rest. In the night I recall waking to find David Miller standing on a chair with a spray bomb in his hand, spraying the transom above the door for the mosquitoes. It seemed that when they came in they would zoom directly for him, but scarcely bothered me. He thought it unfair.

The next morning I went to the local market with Kathy. In the afternoon we went to the leper colony. We also made

The girls' school in Dodoma, Tanzania, where David Miller and I visited my daughter Kathy during our summer 1966 trip to Europe, the Middle East, and Africa.

a visit to the government project where we could see the results of irrigation and proper livestock handling. After nightfall, we were careful to check our path by flashlight so as not to step on any snakes. At night the hyenas howled.

We also visited the school where Kathy taught. There was an opportunity to speak to the girls. We were thrilled to find a local mission Bible school where the leaders of the local villages studied the Bible. Most of these people could neither read nor write, but they learned the Bible by word-of-mouth. I remember we sensed the feeling of the Holy Spirit's presence in their assembly. On Wednesday evening, Kathy and I had a long, late visit. It was so nice to see and visit with our Kathy.

After a good night's rest, we went to Kathy's for breakfast, and after worship together, she and her friend took us to Dodoma to catch the bus. But the bus driver made us go back six miles to the school drive and wait for the bus there. Finally, we saw the bus coming and bade our farewells. We

Several girls at the Dodoma school where our daughter Kathy taught in the 1960s. They are pounding maize in preparation for cooking.

(top) In touring the area around Dodoma, Tanzania, Kathy provided transportation on her "picky-picky."

(bottom) The teachers' residence at Dodoma. This was the cottage where Kathy lived.

started on the long bus ride to Arusha, Uganda.

From Arusha we headed for Munich, Germany, by way of Nairobi and Rome. At the large train depot in Rome, a multitude of people waited for trains. We had difficulty finding someone who spoke our language. We managed to buy our tickets and finally met a lady who spoke German. She was able to tell us when our train would be due. She emphasized the need to be alert when the train came in so we would be sure to get on. "*Sieht das Ihr darufkommt!*" (See that you get on it!), was what she said. Because of her tone, I realized the urgency of the matter.

It was, indeed, a melee when the train came in. Some passengers threw their suitcases and other luggage in through the windows of the train coaches. It was a madhouse.

When we finally did get on the train, we learned we were on the wrong train. Folks had begun to crowd on before the train came to a complete stop. We boarded another train but had no seats. Later another coach was opened, and we got seats for the overnight ride through the Alps.

We spent the next ten days traveling throughout Germany and Switzerland, visiting with friends. We stayed with various of the MCC trainees who had spent time with Anna and me in the 1950s. We also visited some of the German war prisoners who had worked for Glick Plant Farms during World War I.

In West Berlin, we stayed at Friedensheim, a Beachy Amish alternate service program. David Yoder, who was working there at the time, helped us get visas to East Germany. We went to Checkpoint Charley and then south through Leipzig, and on to Buchenwald, a Nazi concentration camp where hundreds of thousands of Jews were murdered during World War II. Here we saw groups of East German youth waiting to see a film on the concentration camp. We entered the camp through the gate by which about 280,000 Jews and others passed to their doom during the years 1937 to 1945. We also saw the furnaces where bodies were cremated. It is frightening to think of the evil.

The evil is past all comprehension. There is too much evil to react to. The experience is numbing. We can be suitably horrified and in awe at the murder of a single person. But how can you react to the murder of millions?

South of Berlin in the East German countryside, we saw beautiful, fruitful land with crops of alfalfa, wheat, and sugar beets. It was time for wheat harvest; one woman was gleaning heads of wheat by hand that had been missed by the machines, in the manner of Ruth in Old Testament days. Obviously, food was still in short supply.

We spent a day in Luxembourg and caught an Icelandic Airways flight for New York. David Miller took a flight to Oklahoma, and I took a bus to Pennsylvania Station and a train to Lancaster. David Miller and I had left Lancaster on June 23, 1966. When I came home, it was August 2, 1966, Ivan's birthday. Truman and Ada Marie and family were visiting from St. Louis.

22.

Several
World Events
Affect Us

The bombing in Vietnam intensified in the 1970s. There was also a lot of herbicide sprayed over the jungle in the hope of removing enemy hiding places. They called it Agent Orange. It was a mixture of 2,4-D and 2,4,5-T. We had used 2,4,5-T on our fencerows in the winter of 1958.

The next summer we had a problem that we never understood until 20 years later when people started talking about Agent Orange. The bred gilts that pastured in the field next to the sprayed fencerow aborted with dead and deformed embroyos. It was puzzling.

When I found out the chemical content and the dangers of Agent Orange, our problem started to make some sense. We found out the brush killer we had used had been accidentally contaminated with something called dioxin during manufacture. It wasn't put in on purpose and the manufacturer may not have been aware of it. But a very small amount of dioxin is all it takes, apparently. Early exposure when an embryo is only a few cells large appears to be more deadly than later when an embryo is near full term.

In Vietnam, American airmen sprayed the stuff over the jungle, often also hitting villages. The villagers used rain-water from their roofs for drinking. Without knowing it, they drank the killer spray. Long after the war, we learned that people became sick and even died as a result of the spraying. Apparently, the dioxin-contaminated 2, 4, 5-T is so deadly that human embryos were aborted instead of being born alive and deformed. Our experience with the hogs would seem to confirm it. 2, 4, 5-T has been taken off the market.

✦ ✦ ✦

1972 marked the first moon landing. American astro-nauts landed on the moon, walked around, and drove their "moon buggy." Since there is no atmosphere on the moon, the buggy could not be equipped with air-inflated tires. They would have blown out. Instead, it was said the moon buggy wheels had built-in springs to cushion shocks.

Some of us found that amusing because in building the shock-absorbing wheels, the NASA engineers re-invented a wheel which a Lancaster Countian named Aaron Horning had been building for the Old Order Amish for some years. When farm equipment was first built with rubber tires, it was easy to convert from rubber back to steel because the axles were plenty strong. But soon designers discovered they could save a lot of money with lighter axles because the air-inflated tires cushioned the shocks on rough ground, rocks, and ditches. That became a problem when the Amish switched the equipment back to steel wheels. Axles and bearings often broke. But the Aaron Horning wheel solved the problem.

Wheels or no wheels, the moon landing seemed an awe-some event. Many doubted that God would permit man to invade the moon. It was said that one Amishman was so convinced that God would not allow it that he told his grandson he'd pay him $1000 if it happened. I never heard if he made good on the promise.

23.

Church-Related Work in the 1970s

Calvary Bible School

In the late 1960s, some of our Beachy Amish people began feeling a need for a winter Bible school, where the youth from all our churches throughout the country could spend several weeks in Bible study. We found a place in Arkansas at Bethel Springs, several miles from Calico Rock. The site included a building formerly used by local Mennonites as a schoolhouse. The building had not been in use for a number of years and was somewhat neglected. But the location was ideal for a boarding school in the Ozarks. It was secluded, with a nice clean stream and a beaver dam.

This was not only a Bible school, but a place where the youth of our churches, would become acquainted with each other and establish friendships. Willie Wagler from Kansas was principal and Ervin Hershberger was his assistant. During the first school term in the winter of 1970, there were two terms of three weeks each. Sixty-six students attended the first term, and there were six teachers along with Wagler and Hershberger. Quite a few people took sick with a mild attack of the flu during the first term. And, our water supply gave out. I think the well caved in.

For me, Bible school was an enriching experience in spite of start-up problems. I had the privilege of meeting other ministers I would not otherwise have learned to know. In the evening after study time, we had many interesting discussions. I don't recall that any of our talks generated heat, even if there were differences of opinion.

Today, after all these years, it is a pleasant experience to meet former students I first learned to know at Calvary Bible School. Travel to and from the school was a problem, especially the first year since no one from Lancaster was going that way. The first year the airports in the east were snowbound during the week I planned to leave for school. Finally there was one flight from Philadelphia to St. Louis on Sunday night. I took that flight. From St. Louis I got a bus to Springfield, Missouri. I was able to get someone from the Hillcrest Home at Harrison, Arkansas (a Beachy Amish Voluntary Service Unit), to come for me at the bus station. The following morning Virgil Kenagy took a group of us to the school. We were late because of the snow. It was apparent that the Arkansas natives were not accustomed to driving in snow.

During the eleven years I was able to participate, 1970-1981, I led both Old and New Testament studies. It was a real joy to relive the experiences of the people in the days of the Old Testament prophets as we studied them together. I also taught a class on the life of the Canadian and Latin American Mennonites, their origin, and their life in the Ukraine during the time of the Czars.

It was a nice experience to teach Bible school those years. *The Calvary Clarion*, the school's paper for 1981, my last year, dedicated one issue in appreciation for my efforts in teaching during those years.

1973 Holy Land Tour

In 1973, I helped Abner Stoltzfus organize a tour for a group of Beachy Amish people who wanted to visit the Holy Land. We had an interesting time together and stopped in Athens, Greece, on the way home.

While there, we had to receive some sort of vaccination. Several days later I became very sick. John U. Lapp and Henry Lapp practically had to carry me around until I got over whatever it was and we were home again.

The Berlin Project

Following World War II, the Beachy Amish churches had started a relief work serving refugees who were coming into Berlin from Russia. Joe and Salome Roth were given charge of that work as agreed upon by the ministers meeting at the Weavertown church in April, 1956. Before the Berlin Wall was built, Voluntary Service workers from the Beachy churches provided biblical teaching for children of the refugee families. That became the nucleus for a Beachy Amish church in Berlin.

Property was purchased in 1957 by the Amish Mennonite Aid Board. AMA was organized as a mission board for the Beachy churches in 1955. The trustees were Jake Hershberger, Elam Kauffman, and Norman Beachy. It was organized as the arm of the church for relief and mission work.

The Berlin work developed into a congregation of 40 members. Because of cultural differences, and the fact that Lewis Overholt was the only pastor, it was considered appropriate for ministers from the United States to visit the Berlin group for counsel and support.

That's how it happened that I went to Berlin in January 1975 and again in January 1978. I also took the opportunity to visit our daughter Kathy who was living in Cardiff, Wales. The congregation in Berlin has since become independent.

Visitors Discover Lancaster County

The tourist influx into Lancaster County which began as a trickle in the mid 1950s reached flood proportions by the

1980s. Every year millions of people come into the County from "the four winds" with questions. After Amish life was featured in several movies, the world discovered these "quaint, colorful peasants who lived in a happy, happy, never-never land" only four hours from New York.

The Lancaster Conference Mennonite church leaders moved to action. They saw an opportunity to share their faith with visitors. It was comprehended as a mission effort. Instead of going to Africa or some other place, they could witness at home.

In the 1960s an information center had been set up in the basement of the Deaf Mennonite Church just north of Route 30 on Witmer Road. This was staffed several days a week by volunteer workers. Later the Information Center was moved to the Mennonite archives along Millstream Road, near Route 30, until a building could be erected specifically for visitors.

At the Mennonite Information Center people who are knowledgeable about the background, beliefs, and practices of the Mennonites and Amish meet the public. They explain the seemingly radical ideas of these people.

The Mennonite Information Center also provides tour guides to accompany visitors through the Amish countryside, to answer questions, and to clarify the Amish way of life.

The Little Red Schoolhouse Information Center

The response of the visitors to the Lancaster Mennonite Information Center witness was accepted as a further challenge. As I remember it, it was the late Daniel Wert and Leslie Hoover who saw the opportunity for an information center at the east end of Lancaster County, for visitors arriving by way of the Pennsylvania Turnpike. Sometime during the late '60s David Blank and Isaac Huyard were made aware of the opportunity. They presented the need to the Weavertown Beachy Amish ministers. The project was approved, and, with the support of the church, a committee was apppointed to pursue the matter.

A little red schoolhouse along Route 23, west of Morgantown, was available and purchased for this work. Floyd Stoltzfus was given the responsibility for coordination with the assistance of others from the three local Beachy Amish congregations. This center has been a Christian witness, supplying information to many visitors during the years.

✦ ✦ ✦

The little red schoolhouse in the Conestoga Valley had a history of its own. According to the late Allen Lee Stoltzfus, during one of the school terms there were 30 pupils and 29 had the last name Stoltzfus. The teacher was a Stoltzfus too, if I remember correctly. All traced their ancestry to the immigrant, Nicholas Stoltzfus who arrived in 1763.

It seems Nicholas, a Lutheran, became acquainted with the Amish as a hired man on an Amish farm in Germany. One thing led to another and he decided he wanted to marry his boss's daughter. There was a problem. The Amish and Mennonites were tolerated only on the condition they not proselytize. The government knew they were harmless and were good farmers, but they were not going to allow them to spread their radical pacifist religion. No way. Anyhow, the local Lutheran pastors probably also disapproved of Stoltzfus's plans to marry the Amish girl.

It was a stand-off. If Nicholas wanted to marry the girl, he first had to join the Amish church. She could perhaps have run off with him and become a Lutheran, but if they had eloped and done something like that, her inheritance could have been in jeopardy and Nicholas apparently was a practical person. He told the local magistrates he wanted to marry the girl because he could not expect any inheritance from his parents. To no avail. He was not granted permission to switch from the Lutheran to the Amish faith.

Nicholas Stoltzfus decided to go ahead and marry his Amish sweetheart. They found their way to America in the 1760s where they could have freedom of religion or freedom from religion, however they wanted it. The Stoltzfus clan has prospered amazingly. That's how it happened an entire schoolhouse full of Stoltzfuses was educated at the little red schoolhouse along Route 23.

One Monday morning during a later school term when Caroline Plank was the teacher, a skunk in the schoolhouse greeted her upon her morning arrival. There was no school that day! It seems the skunk was an unwilling scholar. It had been injected into the school sometime during the weekend. Local pranksters with Amish and Mennonite names were under suspicion because they had bragged about it. If the rumor mill could be credited, the instigating culprit was a Beiler, not a Stoltzfus.

It was said that at the time of World War I there were four farmers, land-joining neighbors, in the valley that had 27 sons, all with the name Stoltzfus. Today about one-fourth of the Amish of Lancaster County have the surname Stoltzfus, and most of the rest are probably related.

Ultimately, the schoolhouse became the Amish visitor information center, staffed by volunteers. I spent some time there in the beginning, but it was a long drive from our home.

Instead, I decided to see whether my help was needed at the Mennonite Information Center on Millstream Road. I became one of the volunteer tour guides in 1972, taking people on a tour of Lancaster County usually in their own cars. I hosted visitors from more than 40 foreign countries and most of the states. It has been one of the most rewarding segments of my 91-year life.

Helping Visitors Understand Amish Beliefs

At the start of a tour I tried to find common ground with the visitors. For example, if the people were Southern Baptists, the place of beginning wasn't quite the same as if they were Orthodox Jews. But in each case there was a common bond. The Baptists were English, but they were influenced by Dutch Mennonite Anabaptists when their movement was formed. It was a place to start in sharing philosophical insights.

And if the guests were Jewish, they already knew about the orientation in Orthodox, Conservative, and Reformed groups. Visitors who were liberal, Reformed Jews often remembered an Orthodox grandmother. The parallels to our Old Order Amish, Beachy Amish, and more liberal Mennonite groupings were easily grasped.

The first hurdle to get over was the term, "Pennsylvania Dutch." I explained that we were not Dutch in the sense of being from The Netherlands. We were Swiss-German. But in the 1700s all Pennsylvania immigrants who spoke any Germanic dialect were called "Dutch." Those from The Netherlands were called "Low Dutch" and the Germans, Alsatians, and Swiss were known as the "High Dutch." They were all Dutchmen to the British who were in control of the government of Pennsylvania. It may have been that the German "Deutsch" is the reason for the English term, "Pennsylvania Dutch," but it doesn't matter as long as we understand what we mean when we use the term.

One must bear in mind that the Amish came here as European peasants before the Industrial Revolution hit. We came out of Switzerland after the Thirty Years War and lived in the Alsace of France and Palatinate of Germany until the migration to America in the 1700s, mostly before the French and Indian War of the mid 1700s.

Amish people lived in Pennsylvania almost a hundred years before most modern inventions became commonplace. In the meantime, we became well-established in life style. As Swiss we were naturally very democratic, so we have always made decisions as a group, not as individuals. We still do. This is the reason we have been able to set limits.

Most Amish groups accept modern technology, but only on our own terms. We refuse to let modern technology take control of our lives. Thereby we are able to hang on to the values and faith we have cherished for over 300 years. But many of us are still Swiss by nature. Like the Swiss, we have little patience with poor workmanship or bad manners.

Beyond that, the Amish and Mennonites believe all children are born innocent and that baptism is only appropriate as a mature, adult decision on the part of the convinced believer. We have the further novel idea that each person is his or her own priest—the priesthood of all believers—which means each member is as capable of prayer and scriptural interpretation as any other. There is no central leader who establishes divine truth. The other item that sets us apart from most other Christians is our insistence on nonresistance. We accept that the New Testament means what it says about the subject. We believe Christians do not fight wars.

24.

Our Family
in the
1970s and '80s

Two things made 1976 memorable for our family. Our son, Jay Elvin, died. He was a beautiful, shockingly intelligent child. When he was just several years old, we marveled at his insight and sense of humor. Then he suddenly stopped talking, became morose, and seemed to turn inward. He had a strange craving for sour things, especially for pickles. Long after he no longer could say any other word, he would say "pickle," but less and less distinctly until he finally stopped speaking at all. He was autistic and epileptic. We tried, even took him to Johns Hopkins, but no medical effort helped. Now he went to be with the Lord. For many years he had not been able to look after himself, so it was with joy that we realized that he was now awaiting us, forever healed.

◆ ◆ ◆

1976 also marked the 50th anniversary of our marriage. Anna's health had deteriorated, but she was able to participate in the event. Our daughter Ada Marie and her husband,

Little Annie Glick, second from the right in the front row. Like other Amish children, she did not speak English when she started school. Anna used to explain, "That made it hard for my teacher" [back row center]. Annie soon learned English, being a quick learner.

Dr. Truman Mast, moved back to Lancaster from the University of Pittsburgh medical school where he had been in research and teaching. With Ada Marie close by to help care for Anna, things became much easier. In her last years Anna wasn't able to look after her house anymore, but with her daughter back to help there was joy.

✦ ✦ ✦

Anna was a very unusual person. Her own mother passed away when she was 16, the oldest of a family of six of whom two were still in diapers. She assumed the role of mother to her little brothers and sisters and was the family homemaker from that day onward. It was a different time. There were few paved roads in rural Iowa. All food except flour, molasses, sugar, and salt was produced at home. She raised the children, grew the food in the garden, put up enough for the

My wife, Anna Glick, at age 16 in 1919. She was a beautiful young woman.

winter, sewed her own clothes, and made clothes for her little brothers and sisters, all without outside help. She made the soap she used to wash their clothes. She even made the yeast she used to bake the family's bread. Her surviving younger sisters remember that she was too proud to cut corners, that their dresses were carefully starched and ironed, and that she braided their hair just before they left for church to make sure they looked very nice.

Actually, Anna had already lived a life and raised one family before we were married. We were both 23 at the time. Creativity and insight were her major strengths. And it was thanks to her creativity and insight that we made it through the Depression. Even when we had little or no money, she

Anna with our daughters, Kathy (right) and Ada Marie (left) in the mid-1950s.

found ways to feed and clothe us and provide support for the less fortunate around us. Anna seldom hesitated. She just stood up and did whatever needed to be done.

When she decided the ladies of the church should have a sewing circle, she went right ahead to help organize it. When the dairy testing association fell apart during World War II because the testers were being drafted, she had a conversation with County Agent "Dutch" Bucher, obtained milk sample bottles, and organized to have them distributed for owner-sampler testing to keep the effort going until the CPS

(Civilian Public Service) testers arrived. When the CPS men came, she put them up as family, for free, until they found places of their own as their wives arrived. At the time, one prominent local dairyman asked who had appointed her to take over. She was surprised by the question since it hadn't occurred to her that she needed to be appointed to do something that obviously needed to be done.

Once, little Ada Marie rolled off the sofa and broke her arm. Anna ran over, picked up the screaming child, and in a flash had set the bone. She cradled the little girl in her arms, and we jumped into our 1936 Ford, rushing to the hospital where the doctors x-rayed Ada Marie's arm. When the doctor examined the x-ray, he said the bone was set so well that he wouldn't mess with it. But it wasn't quite perfect. Ada Marie's one arm was always slightly crooked where it had been broken.

Once, when we didn't have money for a better car and the upholstery on the doors was badly worn, she just took the door panels apart and re-upholstered them. Because she wouldn't let talent go to waste if any help was in sight, she enlisted her 13-year-old son Ivan to help her. He protested that they didn't know how to take car doors apart. But she reassured him, "We'll pay attention to how they're made when we take them apart; then we can put them together again." That's how it worked. I doubt if she really believed there was anything she couldn't handle. Because she was so very capable, she never really understood that others might not be able to do everything if they really wanted to. I suppose less capable people were sometimes intimidated. In any case, I don't see how we'd have made it without her.

Anna died in April 1977 from a stroke after being in a coma for a week. During this time, we continued to talk to her. At our last time together, very near her home-going, Kathy was home from Wales, so Kathy, Ada Marie, and I stood by her bedside. After having a precious goodbye prayer, we noticed a tear as the only response she could give. It was her goodbye. Ivan was with her when she passed away.

After she was gone, I found I was slowing down. Except for church-related activities, I was spending more time with visitors who stopped at the Mennonite Information Center. This involvement became a blessing for me.

In February 1978, Lena Beiler and I were married at the Pequea church by bishop John Glick of the Mine Road church.

A Party for Me in 1983

I turned 80 in 1983. On the occasion Ada Marie and Ivan invited our friends to come by on Sunday afternoon. Ada Marie had expected there might be a bunch. She prepared cake and ice cream for 400 and nearly that many came. The farm was a congested traffic jam. It was humbling but joyous to observe the evidence of friendship that surrounded me. When it was all over and the people had gone home again, I told Lena and the children that the experience was sort of like being the corpse at a viewing. But in the meantime there was more living ahead of us.

Tragedy Strikes Our Family

In January 1986 our daughter Ada Marie had a bad fall at the age of 52. She died instantly, leaving four children, Pamela, Susan, Douglas, and John. Only Ivan and Kathy remain of our family. The loss of Ada Marie seemed almost too much to bear. Many of us had come to depend on her emotional support, in and beyond the family. It was only after she was gone that we discovered how many people depended on her. Then it became apparent why she had a long extension cord on her kitchen telephone. When one came to her house, she would be doing her kitchen work with the telephone cradled on her left shoulder.

It turned out that there were a lot of people who expected she would call them every day; people whom she knew to be in need of emotional support. Her passing left a distressing void, an emptiness that is still there and painful after all these years. Recently one woman, nearly in tears, observed it seemed that she had been supporting the whole world all by herself. Still we go on, somehow. We seek the Lord's will and purpose for our existence.

Fortunate Years

In my 91 years there have been many disappointments and heartaches, but also much joy. I recall it all with rejoicing. Now that they're past, I give thanks for the disappointments and heartaches because they helped me learn to live at peace with myself and my circumstances. To find contentment. And joy.

As the years pass I grow frailer and less fascinated by the events around me. But looking back, I find that with the Psalmist I have to say, "My lines have fallen in pleasant places." They have been fortunate years.

About the Author

Aaron S. Glick has lived in Lancaster County, Pennsylvania, for more than 90 years. Born and raised on an Amish farm in the village of Smoketown, he eventually joined the Beachy Amish church as an adult.

He and his wife, Anna, raised their own family on a rural farm off Rockvale Road. In 1953, Aaron was ordained to the ministry at the Weavertown Beachy Amish church. He spent the next 30 years of his life actively supporting and providing leadership to the church while still operating a busy farm with the help of his wife and family.

Now retired, Aaron and his second wife Lena still live on the Rockvale Road farm, which is managed by his son Ivan.